ADVANCE PRAISE

"Having read Bill's work early, I am struck by how he blends passion with practicality, making personal finance approachable for all ages. His insights don't just inform but transform. In a world where financial literacy is more critical than ever, Bill's guidance provides life-changing clarity and a roadmap to financial freedom. This isn't just a book; it's a toolkit for thriving—don't just read it; live it!"

> – Dave Nordel, CMSgt, USAF (ret), RN, BSN, MS, CHEP,
> *Military Transition Coach,*
> *Keynote Motivational Speaker & Leadership Coach,*
> *and CEO of Vet READY and MaxFab Consulting*

"Bill Haase has handed us a mirror to reflect on our relationship with money and a roadmap to take control of it. He's provided a wake-up call for anyone struggling with money. He blends raw honesty with practical wisdom, challenging the way we think about money rather than just telling us what to do with it. His insights on financial habits, emotional spending, and generational money beliefs make this a must-read at a time when financial literacy is needed more than ever.

Bill has walked the same road as his readers. His passion for helping people break free from financial overwhelm is evident on every page. If you've ever felt like money controls you more than you control it, this book is for you."

> – Connor Tyson, ChFC ® Chartered Financial Consultant,
> *Personal Financial Coach, and*
> *Owner/Founder of Progress Solutions LLC*

Our
Mindset
on Money

It's Easy to Control,
So Why Don't We?

BILL HAASE

Our Mindset on Money: It's Easy to Control, So Why Don't We?
Published by Money Mindset Media LLC
Lake Villa, Illinois, U.S.A.

HAASE, BILL, Author
OUR MINDSET ON MONEY
BILL HAASE

Library of Congress Control Number: 2025901174

ISBN: 979-8-9924427-0-0, 979-8-9924427-2-4 (paperback)
ISBN: 979-8-9924427-3-1 (hardcover)
ISBN: 979-8-9924427-1-7 (digital)

BUSINESS & ECONOMICS / Personal Finance / Budgeting
YOUNG ADULT NONFICTION / Personal Finance
SELF-HELP / Personal Growth / Success

Publishing Management: Susie Schaefer (finishthebookpublishing.com)
Editing: April Rust (https://truepenediting.com)
Book Design: Michelle M. White (mmwbooks.com)
Cover illustration derived from image by peshkova at stock.adobe.com

QUANTITY PURCHASES: Schools, companies, professional groups, clubs, and other organizations may qualify for special terms when ordering quantities of this title. For information, email info@moneymindsetmedia.com

MONEY MINDSET MEDIA LLC

Bill in his trading jacket from the '90s
... it still fits!

This book is dedicated to
my brothers and sisters from the Eurodollar pit
at the Chicago Mercantile Exchange.
Thanks for the ride!

Table of Contents

Preface

LET ME ASK YOU SOMETHING, DO YOU LIVE YOUR LIFE WITH intent, or by default?

The reality is you probably live both ways, but what part is with intent versus what part is by default? This book is for the many of you who live life by default financially, with a focus on young adults. There's very little education on how to deal with money as an individual person unless you make that your pursuit in life. As we grow up, we're sheltered by our parents from many of the harsh realities of life, until we head out into the real world and learn on our own. Life lessons happen at all ages, but learning how to deal with money is very elusive in that we simply don't talk about subjects we don't understand. One thing I learned as a financial advisor is that most spouses don't talk about money to each other, and therefore are unable to pass along much wisdom to their children. This perpetuates from generation to generation, and most of us wind up being controlled by—instead of taking control of—our financial situation.

I'm as guilty as anyone in not teaching more to my children. And I've been through the financial ringer like most everyone else. I've been broke many times and even lost my home in the housing bubble. I have struggled throughout my life with money, and I know more than many about it. My father said he could never understand how money has never motivated me, and yet, that's the only business I've ever been in. This book is about taking control of your finances and understanding your relationship with money, not about what to do with it. I find it interesting that it's the one thing we're not supposed to talk about and yet affects every aspect of our lives.

Talking about money has always been taboo in our society. We don't tell anyone how much we get paid in our job (especially someone we work with), and we don't discuss how we use it. In fact, *we* don't even like knowing how we use it because we know we waste more than we're willing to admit. And we don't talk about things we know little about because we don't like to come across as unintelligent. Add that to it being taboo to talk about and we get the perfect storm in which money then controls us.

We look at money being the solution to all our troubles and rarely at it being the root of them. People will lie, cheat, steal, and even kill for money and yet still not be satisfied because they don't know what to do with it other than spend it. Spending is easy, while earning is hard, and we learn better how to spend than earn because that's how our brain works. We are more pleased when spending, while earning just doesn't stimulate us. So, our behavior changes between these two aspects of life, and therefore our ability to see and adapt is limited.

This leads us to the fact that most of us live paycheck to paycheck because we have this insatiable appetite to spend it as fast as we make it, and then some. Let's face it, for those of you who get a bonus each year, I would bet that before you even know how much it is, you've already thought about how you're going to spend it. Or when it's time to do your taxes and you know you'll be getting a return, you already know it's faster to file online and have that refund directly deposited to your bank account. And you've already figured out how you're going to spend it. It's what we've been trained to do.

I have been "called" to teach and preach all about financial literacy to those who seek to take control of their lives and their money. It's really not hard to do, though it does take some effort. I know, I know, you say, how can money be easy to control when I've been around it all my life and I've never been able to realize any control? We have been psychologically conditioned to spend. When we're young, we get trained in ways to spend before we ever learn how to save, and when we're old, our biggest fear is running out of money, but do we stop spending? It never seems to stop being a concern in life.

This book was written to help you understand your relationship with money, take control of it, and enjoy more of what life has to offer. This is not about how to do a budget (although I do show that) or a guide to what you should be doing with every penny. It's more about your mindset and how you can gain control and then realize healthier relationships, reduce stress, increase productivity, enjoy your time with others, and live life more freely. Life is an expensive ordeal where money plays a role, starting from conception, and is with us through death. Yet so many do so little to learn more about it and how it affects them.

Some would say I'm trying to do something that can't be done: change your behaviors or beliefs. In reality, we change our behaviors and beliefs all the time as we gain more experience and knowledge. This book is about recognizing your current financial behaviors and providing you with the opportunity to make simple changes that could have a profound effect on how you live. Once you become aware, you can then gain control.

If you only read the first chapter, you'll be on your way to greater financial freedom.

"What you are not aware of, you are a slave to. What you are aware of, you control."

– Anthony de Mello,
Indian Jesuit priest/psychotherapist

one

Take Control

THE FUNNY THING ABOUT MONEY IS THAT IT'S SURPRISINGLY easy to learn how to take control of your financial situation—if you truly want to. So, let me ask you: What is the one thing that constantly poses a problem in life? It's the one thing that is always there, from childhood until death. Relationships and material things may come and go, but money remains a constant factor. Yet, we often avoid taking just a little time from our busy lives to learn more about it.

As T. Harv Eker, best-selling author of *Secrets of the Millionaire Mind* and *SpeedWealth*, once said, "The number one problem in today's generation and economy is the lack of financial literacy." In reality, people from all backgrounds and generations lack this crucial skill. However, many are eager to understand how money works and how to control it.

From my experience as a former financial advisor, one thing stands out: Couples rarely talk about money—or sex.

I used to joke that I could help with one of those topics. But the truth is, if couples aren't discussing money with each other, they certainly aren't talking about it with their children. This lack of conversation perpetuates a cycle of financial ignorance from generation to generation, allowing those who understand money to exploit those who don't.

Consider this: Financial habits are shaped early, from the way products are advertised and positioned to the encouragement of credit use. When a child goes to college, they often receive a debit card funded by their parents, teaching them how to spend without understanding the consequences. Once they graduate, the card disappears, but the habits remain. They get a job, sign up for a credit card, and, a month later, a bill arrives—an unplanned expense without a budget to cover it. How could they have planned for it given they were never taught to budget in the first place? Oh sure, every time you called home asking for more money, your parents would tell you that you should learn to budget your money better. The same ones who don't budget themselves, most likely.

MINDSET

Your mindset toward money plays a crucial role in how you manage it. Many of us have inherited beliefs and attitudes about money from our families, cultures, and personal experiences. Recognizing and understanding these beliefs is essential to making conscious financial decisions. Here in America, we learn to spend what we make as soon as we make it. The reality is, 66–78 percent of Americans live paycheck to paycheck, not necessarily because they earn so little but because they've developed a habit of spending as they earn.

Think about it: When you receive a big raise or bonus, what typically happens? Most people splurge, and within weeks or months, it's all gone. In fact, about 70 percent of people who win a lottery or get a big windfall actually end up broke in just a few years, according to the National Endowment for Financial Education. I once belonged to the NFL Alumni Association of Illinois (no I did not play in the NFL) in hopes I could help ex-players learn how to handle all that money they earned. Problem was, very few had much of anything left after a few years. Let's face it—spending money is more enjoyable than earning it for most of us. But why do we have this insatiable urge to spend every dollar we make, and often more? It's about status. We're obsessed with living the best life and showing off to those around us. Where we live, the size of our home, the flashy car, and fancy clothes all represent who we want to be perceived as. What I have a tough time understanding is how we believe that people who appear to have lots of money are also very smart. I spent twenty years in the trading pits of Chicago and have met many people who did very well financially yet weren't the brightest bulbs in the pack. Though there were many who believed that about themselves.

As you get older, you'll look back at all the meaningless things you spent money on—cars, homes, clothes, jewelry, and countless items to fill those homes and cars, or the shopping sprees at Nordstrom and those iconic blue boxes from Tiffany's. And don't even get me started on diamonds. Did you know they lose 25-50 percent of their value upon resale? As Nicky Oppenheimer, chair of De Beers, once said, "Diamonds are intrinsically worthless, except for the deep psychological need they fill." After all, we've learned that you better put a ring on it.

As I write this in 2024, household debt in the US has reached an all-time high. Americans began the year with a staggering $17.3 trillion in debt, including mortgages, credit cards, auto loans, student loans, and other liabilities. Meanwhile, wages have only seen a slight increase, with median weekly earnings rising by just 3.5 percent year over year, according to MarketWatch. Remember, we all face fixed, variable, and incidental costs. If you're relying more on credit, your monthly payments will increase (under the variable costs), leaving even less money for incidental expenses. Worse, you may find yourself deciding which bills to pay and which to put off.

Feel the stress creeping in? Money itself doesn't create stress—how you manage it does. If you're not financially savvy and continue to live by default, that stress will only grow. The thing is, it's your choice how you live your life, and most of us choose not to understand money. It's like any other subject that starts off fairly simple and as you go along can get more difficult to understand. But you need to start somewhere.

FINANCIAL HABITS

Tracking your spending is simple and takes little time, but it can reveal a lot about your relationship with money and spending habits. We all have fixed costs like rent or mortgage, car payments, streaming subscriptions, and insurance along with variable expenses such as utilities, credit card payments, groceries, entertainment, gas, and clothing. Since we usually know our income, it's easy to figure out what's left for incidental spending.

This is where you truly learn about yourself and your money habits. It's also the category that many people prefer to ignore. Do you really want to know how much you spend on coffee or online purchases you don't need? The "incidentals" category shows you how you spend the money left after covering your basic living expenses. It reveals whether you have control over your money or whether your money controls you.

Fixed and variable costs play a role, but beyond credit card debt (which is a choice), it's the incidentals that reveal how much your spending is driven by emotion and spontaneity. Marketers and sales professionals understand these habits well and design strategies to exploit them. Ever see an ad that says you know you want this, we have it right now, and we'll even finance it for you? How can one resist when there's zero out-of-pocket expense?

Reflect on your past financial decisions. What were the outcomes? What would you do differently now? For example, my son once bought an expensive car he loved, but after a couple of years, he decided to sell it to reduce his financial burden and bought a used car at half the cost. I commend him for making that tough decision that reduced his financial pressure and taught him valuable lessons about making wiser financial choices in the future. We all have wants, and you can fulfill many of them if you learn to budget and plan. But more often than not, we don't.

One of the biggest jokes in the financial advising industry is that people spend more time planning and budgeting for their next vacation than they do for their retirement. And when was the last time you went on vacation and stayed within your budget? I'm not speaking to the few who do but to the majority who don't.

When I was eleven, my family went on a two-week ski trip. On the very first day, I lost one of my skis over a steep incline, making it impossible to retrieve. Do you think my parents planned for that? With thirteen days left on the trip, they faced an unexpected expense for a new set of skis. It was an accident, but such things happen all the time. As any insurance agent will tell you, "Life happens," and it's true.

IMPORTANCE OF FINANCIAL LITERACY

Understanding your money is crucial to eliminating the stress of constantly struggling to balance your finances. Once you learn where and how you spend, you'll begin to question your purchasing decisions. Over time, you'll become an expert at knowing what you want and how to achieve it.

As mentioned, my research shows that 66–78 percent of Americans live paycheck to paycheck (according to MarketWatch and Forbes). This indicates that many people lack control over their money and spending habits. Certainly, some individuals are in challenging situations—they may not earn enough to cover their cost of living when inflation rears its ugly head, they face health-related hardships, or they have low-paying jobs. However, there are also those who drive expensive cars costing more than their rent or mortgage or live in homes that are too large and costly to maintain.

I've seen people who earn substantial incomes yet remain broke because their money is entirely tied up in debt. According to CNBC, more than half of Americans making over $100,000 a year live paycheck to paycheck. This brings to mind shows like *Airplane Repo* where they seize planes, boats, and other assets from people who seem entitled to their luxury toys but struggle to pay for them. These are individuals who do not have control over their finances or their spending habits.

The lesson here is simple: It doesn't matter how much money you make; what truly matters is how effectively you use it.

UNDERSTANDING MONEY MANAGEMENT

While the benefits of managing money are numerous, one thing I've learned from friends who teach financial literacy to company employees is that there are additional advantages. Companies have found that providing financial education for their employees not only improves productivity and retention but also makes them happier when they are no longer worrying about money.

- **Reduced Stress:** Knowing how to manage your money decreases financial stress.
- **Improved Health:** Financial stability promotes overall well-being and reduces anxiety.
- **Better Relationships:** Money is a common source of conflict in relationships. The baby boomer generation was the first to experience a significant rise in dual-income households, but they also witnessed the damage caused when one spouse loses a job or has their hours reduced. This can be particularly challenging when a household has grown accustomed to a higher income level. We've all experienced it: You get a big raise, and soon you're enjoying more of life's pleasures, which often means spending more, not saving more.

Consider shows like *Pawn Stars* where people come in to sell items they believe hold great value. Notice how every person talks about how they plan to spend the money, rarely about saving or investing it. Financial literacy helps you navigate these challenges, ultimately making your life more enjoyable. Knowing where your money is can provide some comfort, but understanding why it is where it is brings even greater peace of mind.

As a "recovering" financial advisor, I found it difficult to manage the portfolios of clients who didn't understand why they were invested in certain products—whether inherited from a previous advisor or chosen by me. I would always explain the purpose of each investment and its place in the overall plan (a discussion that should occur before considering any investment). However, many people don't like to admit they feel clueless, so they nod in agreement even when they don't fully understand.

It's okay not to know everything about a subject—whether it's cars, health, or money. Yet, for some reason, when it comes to finances, we often don't want to reveal just how little we know. But acknowledging our gaps in financial knowledge is the first step toward gaining control over our money.

PERCEPTION

There's a deceptive force that often sits on our shoulder, whispering in our ear at just the right moment. It's the voice that tells us to ignore that sinking feeling in our stomach or the unease welling up in our gut because we know what we're about to do will hurt us financially. This force is called perception.

(There's much more to this "gut" feeling than you know, but trusting it is a good thing.)

We all want to be seen as smart and wealthy, and if we're not, we often try to create the perception that we are. This mindset directly affects how we spend money, and you may already see it in your own life. The house, the car, the clothes, jewelry, shoes, golf clubs, haircuts—everything can become about perception. Needing to be perceived as wealthier than we are is a financial trap that can devastate us over time.

And the hardest part about perception? It works. We often believe those who appear smarter and wealthier than us are, simply because they look the part.

Why do so many people listen to actors, singers, or entertainers about who should be our next president or about global warming? Why trust politicians to know anything about money? Two reasons: perception and laziness. They appear successful and wealthy, so we assume they know what they're talking about. It's easier than doing our own research and making informed decisions. Perception and laziness are the tools used to drain money from us every day in countless ways.

Consider the example of electric vehicles (EVs). You might be able to list the positives of owning an EV, but can you also list the negatives? Some of you might know a few, but most don't. We often take the easy route, believing what we see on TV, social media, or in ads. Even if you don't see yourself as a salesperson, you've been in sales all your life. Every day, you sell the status you want others to perceive in you, never mentioning your flaws. The same goes for advertising.

Are you starting to see how easy it is to be manipulated? This goes beyond just money—it touches every part of life.

How much do you know about the medications you take? You trust your doctor, so you might forget to ask about side effects, the duration of treatment, or even the cost. I've made the same mistake. In 2009, I needed a hip replacement and rushed into the decision. My doctor suggested a titanium hip, "perfect" for someone active like me. Without doing my homework, I agreed. Later, I discovered that this type of hip had caused complications for others. Within a few years, I developed cluster headaches due to metal from the hip entering my bloodstream. When I finally researched the issue, I found numerous negative reports. In 2019, I had the hip replaced with a ceramic one and haven't had any problems since.

Do I blame the doctor? Not really. He was "sold" on the titanium hip just like I was, having been told only the positives. Neither of us did our homework, and it cost me years of pain, time, and money. This experience shows how pervasive the temptation to take the easy route can be. We don't often learn from the consequences of our decisions; we just decide to trust those who seem to know more than we do.

We could debate all day about a doctor's responsibility, but this is about taking ownership of our own choices. Financial literacy, like any other knowledge, is about making informed decisions and understanding the true costs—not just financially but in every aspect of our lives. Here's an actual cost you can understand: You buy a car for $30,000, and it's going to cost you $400 per month for the next four years. That's $400 per month you no longer have available to spend on anything else, *for forty-eight months.* I hope this makes you think in a different way about how you spend.

One other thing I'd like to bring up about how lazy we can be: For every scam artist out there who takes our money, they are not solely to blame. They were able to take our money because we believed what we were told and did not do our homework to make sure it was a solid investment. And the problem gets bigger when we realize we may be getting scammed but are afraid to find out the truth. We may even be conned into investing more in the hopes that it isn't the scam our gut is telling us it really is. Greed is a killer of many dreams.

TOOLS AND RESOURCES

There are many ways to learn about managing your finances, depending on your preferred style. However, sometimes the simplest approach is best—the KISS method ("Keep It Simple, Stupid"). Start by writing out your expenses on a piece of paper or on a spreadsheet. Begin with your monthly income at the top, then list your fixed costs (expenses that are the same every month), followed by variable costs (expenses that occur every month but vary in amount), and finish with the incidentals (all other expenses).

- **Books and Newsletters:** There are numerous excellent books on personal finance and free newsletters that provide valuable insights and tips. I don't provide specific ones as we all have different ways we absorb knowledge, and you can find what works best for you with a little effort. Get what I'm trying to do here?

- **Online Courses and Resources:** Websites like QuickBooks, Coursera, and Udemy offer courses and tools on personal finance and investing. Most banks also provide resources to attract your attention, often with the intent to sell products or services—so be cautious.
- **Financial Blogs and Podcasts:** Following reputable financial blogs and listening to podcasts can help you stay informed and motivated. But if the main aspect of the people hosting the show is based on selling you something, move on to another option.
- **Seek Advice from Trusted Individuals:** Ask those around you who seem financially responsible about whom they consult or what they do. However, remember that what works for one person may not necessarily work for another.

I've met many people who say they were on a specific program designed to help them get out of debt and gain full ownership of their home. These programs often promise that you'll be debt free within a certain time frame. Ironically, many of the people I'd spoken with were still in debt and hadn't paid off their homes well past that time frame, yet they continued to pay for the service and believed in it. When I asked how they felt about their progress, I often got no response. Just like the folks who register with an online school program and never complete it. They believe they'll get back to it at some point, so they keep paying. At the bachelor's level, primarily online colleges report relatively low graduation rates compared to other types of colleges. According to Forbes Advisor, just over 20 percent of undergraduate students enrolled at primarily online colleges earn their bachelor's degrees within six years. Belief is so strong that we often can't see the truth.

There are many folks who believe strongly about a certain supplement (which is not regulated like a drug is) that will help you regain memory loss. I was looking at taking the Series 7 exam and hoping for some help. But after doing a quick online search, I learned there's no real proof of the product doing anything it claims to do. There's one small study that is inconclusive, and there's no study on the long-term effects it may have. I don't know about you, but I don't want to put something in my body when I have no clue about the long-term effects.

CHANGING YOUR FINANCIAL MINDSET

Are you feeling bored yet? Still thinking this is simply basic budgeting that you already know but have no desire to actually do? Maybe you believe you always know how much you have and what you can or cannot afford. Let me tell you about an experience I had while mentoring some high school students on building a business. One of them asked if I could teach more about the financial aspects. I explained that we'd have to start with basic personal financial literacy before moving up to business finances, as there are both similarities and key differences between the two.

To illustrate, I asked a few of the students a simple question: How do you know how much money is in your bank account? The answers ranged from "I go to the ATM, and it tells me" to "I know when I run out because I get an email saying I'm overdrawn." Parents, take note—if you help your children open a bank account, please show them how to use and manage it properly. I'm often asked what parents can do to teach financial literacy to their young children. My advice is always the same: In the first year, just teach them to save. This is the best foundation anyone can have. Chores and allowances are a good start, but focus on instilling the habit of saving. Trust me, they'll learn how to spend soon enough, and hopefully, they'll put more thought into how spending affects their savings efforts.

Changing your financial mindset means reprogramming your thoughts and beliefs about money. This can be done through budgeting, education, self-reflection, and consistent practice. Don't tell me it's too hard or that you don't understand numbers—you know exactly what you're earning, spending, and when you're running low on money. Taking just thirty minutes a month to review your budget can be life changing.

Did you know that 50 percent of people in America cannot afford an unexpected $400 expense? I can almost guarantee you will face an expense like that every year. Consider this: We're expecting twenty-five major storms to hit the

US this year (double the usual number), which means your homeowners, car, and/or rental insurance is likely going up. Mine went up 42 percent this year. A neighbor friend mentioned to me he was not happy about his insurance rates going up because we have to pay for the hurricanes that hit other states but will never hit ours. Insurance companies have a thing about paying out billions of dollars in damages without knowing how they're going to recover it. Or think about the appliance that decides to die at the worst possible time, or the car that fills your garage floor with oil. Maybe it's a flooded basement, a broken fence, or a pet that gets hit by a car. I recently discovered that a massive oak tree in my backyard—almost dead—would cost $3,500 to remove. I didn't plan for that expense, and I'm still hoping Mother Nature helps it fall away from my home, not into it. Who wants to spend $3,500 on taking down a tree? But remember, "Life happens."

Changing your financial mindset isn't just about managing money better—it's about preparing for the unexpected and taking control of your financial future.

EDUCATE YOURSELF

My friend J. W. Wilson said in his book *Cracking the Learning Code*, "You can't make changes you don't know how to make."

By conducting a monthly assessment of your expenditures, you'll start to recognize patterns and develop a greater sense of control over your finances. You may identify areas where you can cut costs, such as reducing credit card debt, moving into more affordable housing, or selling an expensive car. One effective approach is to analyze your expenses as a percentage of your income. While the results might be uncomfortable, this insight can guide your future financial decisions. Remember, there is no perfect way to control every expense; what's more important is understanding how you spend and the relationship you have with money. Everyone makes poor financial choices at times, but not everyone learns from them.

Stay informed about financial news and trends to make better decisions. For example, pay attention to the cost of groceries, gas, lumber, utilities, and other everyday expenses. This isn't just so you can complain about rising prices, but so you can adjust your spending as needed to minimize the impact. We just had the Federal Reserve reduce interest rates and many folks know that means it's cheaper to borrow money this week than it was last week. Both personal and business decisions are affected by this event dramatically. If you can anticipate potential challenges by being more aware of what's going on around you, you'll be able to make adjustments to ease any potential issues coming your way.

Plan ahead whenever possible. Consider life events like weddings, having children, relocating for a new job, college, or travel. And don't forget about that unique American concept—retirement. I'll dig deeper into that topic later in the book.

SELF-REFLECTION

Regularly assess your financial goals and track your progress. Celebrate your successes and learn from your mistakes. Challenge any negative beliefs you have about money and replace them with positive affirmations and constructive thoughts.

Remember, gaining control over your finances is not an overnight fix—it's a process that takes time. It took years for you to get where you are, and it will take some time to regain control. Everyone has a different learning curve, but I assure you that you will start learning from the very first time you write out your monthly expenses.

I remember a conversation with my mother-in-law after my father-in-law passed away. He had set up a budget for her, and while she initially liked it and said she learned from it, she eventually gave up. When I asked why, she explained that the numbers kept changing and many costs were higher than expected. And that's really the point, to see the changes and make adjustments. The reality is, it's up to you to take control of your finances because, truthfully, everyone else is trying to take your money. To be fair to my mother-in-law, it's true that over time costs of just about everything will go up, and a budget from nine or ten years ago has changed a great deal. Hence, I say to keep an eye on those expenses monthly so you can learn to adjust as needed.

If you don't like what you see when reviewing your budget, take action to change it. Learn from it, and you will feel more empowered. But whatever you do, don't walk away from it as you'll lose control once again.

PRACTICE GOOD FINANCIAL HABITS

Consistently apply what you learn. Create a budget, set financial goals, and regularly track your spending and savings. Make these habits a regular part of your life.

Surround yourself with financially responsible people. Observe their habits and seek advice when needed, but remember, don't just blindly copy what others do—listen, learn, and decide if their approach works for your situation. We've all heard that if we just did what rich people do, we'd become rich ourselves. Wrong! The truth is, if we all had the money that wealthy people have, then maybe we'd have a chance—maybe. Remember, it's not how much we have but what we do with it.

Ask yourself, Do I really need that right now? Try waiting a week or two before making a purchase, especially when something catches your eye. We often buy on impulse, and marketers know this all too well. They strategically place items in stores and use persuasive language to entice impulsive purchases. They know many of us don't practice good financial habits and are skilled at using this against us.

STEPS TO IMPROVE YOUR FINANCIAL MINDSET

Start with small, achievable goals. As you reach them, gradually set more challenging ones. For example, begin by building a savings cushion or paying down debt. Focus on the smallest debt first, then move on to the next, or tackle the debt with the highest interest rate for a more impactful start. I'll discuss these strategies in more detail later in the book.

Understanding your relationship with money is the first step toward taking control of your financial future. By identifying your beliefs and habits, improving your financial literacy, and changing your mindset, you'll be on your way to making better financial decisions and enjoying more of what life has to offer. I promise, once you remove those financial blinders, you'll see so much more in life that you can enjoy.

You've just covered the basics: understanding your relationship with money, how you use it, how it affects you, and what you can do to take control. If this is all you do, you will already have come a long way toward reducing the frustration that comes with the age-old question: Where did my money go?

If you wish to learn more about how money works and how to make it work for you, read on. But fair warning: It will get a bit more complicated—though also more fun if you enjoy numbers. If not, the information will still help you understand more clearly when working with others who explain financial decisions. You don't want to be sitting in a meeting with a planner or advisor nodding along when you have no idea if their plan is right for you. I've been that advisor, watching clients' eyes glaze over as they say they understand and agree, even though I know they don't. That's why I stopped being an advisor and turned my passion toward helping people like you grasp financial literacy—so you can make informed decisions based on real understanding.

Imagine how empowering it would feel to truly understand your investments and know how your money is working for you.

This book isn't designed to give you all the ins and outs of credit, banking, insurance, and investing. Instead, it's here to provide you with the basics to help you make better decisions. One of my company's mission statements was "We provide knowledge, knowledge gives you options, and options give you freedom."

BASIC CHECKLIST TO GET YOU STARTED

PERSONAL BUDGET

1. **Monthly Income:**

2. **Monthly Fixed Costs:**
    - Mortgage/rent
    - Property taxes (if applicable)
    - Car payments
    - Insurance premiums
    - Cable/internet
    - Streaming services
    - Other loan payments
    - Phone bills

- Utilities (if on a fixed plan)
- Homeowners' association fees
- Club membership fees
- Lawn maintenance

3. **Monthly Variable Costs:**
    - Credit card payments
    - Utilities (if not on a fixed plan)
    - Groceries
    - Gas for car
    - Clothing/personal care
    - Entertainment
    - Medical bills
    - Home/car repairs and maintenance
    - Hobbies

4. **Monthly Incidental Costs:**
    - Service fees
    - Tipping
    - Parking/tolls
    - All unplanned expenses

5. **Savings:**
    - Savings account
    - Retirement accounts (IRA/ROTH/401(k)/403(b))
    - Investments
    - Home equity
    - Other assets

This exercise is not just about listing the obvious expenses; it's about gaining a deeper understanding of how you view and use money. It helps you recognize patterns and influences that affect your financial situation and identify areas for improvement. By doing so, you'll also learn to understand your business financials, spotting trends you can capitalize on, or avoiding potential negative impacts.

Use this checklist as a tool to visualize your financial landscape, make informed decisions, and better manage your resources going forward. Don't think of it as just telling you where you spend your money; that's not what the exercise is about.

two

Setting Financial Goals

YOU CAN'T MAKE CHANGES YOU DON'T KNOW HOW TO make! Thank you J. W.

Just like goals in life, at work, or in your business, setting financial goals is essential for managing your finances effectively. Whether you're saving for a significant purchase, paying off debt, building wealth for the future, or all the above, well-defined financial goals provide direction and motivation. This guide will help you navigate the process of setting and achieving your financial objectives.

IDENTIFY YOUR PRIORITIES

1. **Short-Term Goals (0–1 year):** Build an emergency fund, plan a vacation, handle minor home or car repairs, or save for special life events—like a family member's wedding in the Bahamas next summer.

2. **Medium-Term Goals** (1–5 years): Purchase a car, save for a house down payment, pay off significant debts, or start a family. While it might not be common to think, "We're financially stable enough to have kids," it's important to consider this aspect of life. Costs increase once you have children, and for many, they never stop. In fact, CNN reported that 59 percent of baby boomers still support their adult children financially to some extent.

3. **Long-Term Goals** (5+ years): Plan for retirement, fund your children's education, or pay off a mortgage and other debt. These years often require the most effort, as education and retirement typically represent the largest financial needs. It's easy to feel relieved when kids finish college and you no longer need to fund their education—unless, of course, they decide to pursue a master's or PhD. While a college degree correlates with higher earnings over a lifetime, the upfront cost isn't always worth it. The value depends on career choices, life goals, and the necessity of taking on student loans. Keep in mind that the longer you're in school the less time you have to earn income, and you may have greater debt to be paid off when your education is completed.

ASSESS YOUR CURRENT FINANCIAL SITUATION

Understand where you stand financially right now—this is your starting point. Create a budget to get a clear picture of your monthly financial situation. A budget will help identify trends, like overspending, allowing you to devise a plan to move forward and monitor your progress. While budgeting may seem like a chore, it becomes routine over time. Soon, you'll start to see the positive impact it has as you follow your plan. Even if you prefer living life spontaneously, ignoring your finances will eventually catch up with you. This book isn't about dictating what you should or shouldn't do—it's about offering ways to minimize the financial challenges that money can bring. Since money is a constant throughout life, why not take control of it?

BE SPECIFIC

Instead of vague goals like "I want to save money," be specific: "I want to save $10,000 for a down payment on a house in three years" or "I need to set aside $200 per month for our next vacation." Methods like the 80/10/10, 60/20/20, or 50/30/20 rules based on percentages of income to spend on fixed, variable, and incidental costs and savings can help allocate your income, but they may not suit everyone as costs and income change. Remember, the cheapest thing you can pay for is attention—once you start tracking your spending, financial decisions become easier. And that's the point.

SET MEASURABLE GOALS

Incorporate your financial goals into your budget. If you want to save a specific amount per week, month, or year, add a line to your budget sheet to track your progress. Even small savings add up over time—for instance, saving $20 per weekly paycheck can amount to over $1,000 annually. Consider opening an investment account to grow your savings, depending on your risk tolerance. For those who prefer minimal risk, an online bank with higher interest rates could be a good option, but remember, that inflation can impact purchasing power. If inflation (cost of living) is running at 5 percent per year, that means you need to make that much to maintain the same level of value for your money. Meaning $100 at the beginning of the year with a 5 percent inflation rate equals $95 purchasing power at the end of that year. You lost 5 percent of value because the cost of living went up by 5 percent. I'll dive deeper into this later.

CREATE A FINANCIAL PLAN

Allocate a portion of your income toward each financial goal. Start small if you're young but increase your contributions as you get older and your earning power grows because the burden becomes greater and requires more resources to catch and keep up. Consistency is key—keep the same percentages going into each goal as your income grows. This approach helps prevent situations like those faced by many baby boomers where 45 percent have no retirement savings, and 28 percent of those who do have less than $100,000 saved.

Use budgeting tools or apps to monitor your progress. While it's possible to manage your finances alone, many people benefit from professional advice.

BUILD AN EMERGENCY FUND

Before pursuing other goals, establish an emergency fund with three to six months' worth of living expenses (some advisors recommend six to twelve months). I know you hear this all the time, and I hope you never need to tap into this fund, but the likelihood of never having to is almost zero in my estimation and experience. Now you may be learning you don't need to hit the coffee shop every day or that impulse buy you put back since you know you don't really need it. Have you ever gone to the grocery store and bought only what you needed? This fund is a safety net for unexpected expenses, job loss, or rising inflation costs, those subtle cost increases that can quietly eat into your budget. Keep growing or maintaining this fund to stay financially secure. Rising costs of things like gas and groceries are painful, but they aren't killing you. What's killing you is your inability to adjust when rising costs occur, and they will always occur. Can you think of anything that costs less than it did ten or twenty years ago?

MANAGE DEBT

This is a big one because this is the one that gets us into trouble. Debt management is critical to achieving financial stability. Prioritize paying off high interest debts first. There are two common strategies:

- **Snowball Method:** Pay off the smallest debts first while making minimum payments on larger debts. The money from each paid-off debt is rolled into the next, creating a snowball effect.
- **Avalanche Method:** Focus on paying off debts with the highest interest rates first to save on interest and get out of debt faster.

Are you overwhelmed by debt and it's draining you of any excess funds and you feel like there's no way out? I have known many people that get into this situation, and there are options. None are great, but all work in the end.

Just watch TV. Eventually you'll see a debt-reduction commercial that claims they will get you out of debt within a certain time frame, and they can. But you need to do your homework as this method works much like a bankruptcy option. It will stay on your credit report for up to seven years, which will affect your borrowing power. Another option may be to take out a loan that covers all your credit card debt, car loan, and debts other than a mortgage. This loan payment should be lower than the payments of those combined loans for it to be beneficial. It will reduce your monthly expenses, but it will not be as low a monthly pay-ment as the debt-reduction/consolidation folks. However, it also won't carry that seven-year credit report hit. In the end, you need to decide what's best for you, and keep in mind that the goal is to eliminate as much debt as you can, as quickly as you can. None of these actions will ruin your life, but taking no action will only add to the stress.

Once you've decided the course of action you are going to take, you will now need to make sure you monitor the prog-ress. You'll think I'm crazy, but this is where it gets fun. As you pay down your debt, you will start feeling relief, which leads to thinking about what you can do in the future. Yes, *hope* comes back to life! But remember to stay on track as best you can, allow for adjustments as you plan forward, and celebrate your efforts. I don't mean head out and buy a new Porsche, but maybe a nice dinner. Will it all be smooth sailing, no. There will be times where you get off the path and have to reel yourself back in. It's okay, life happens.

SEEK PROFESSIONAL ADVICE

Admit that money might not be your area of expertise. And like most people, numbers may bore you to death. We all have a gift or a talent that we bring to the table. He's great at managing others or she's a genius with marketing, or that person is a great CEO. How about that electrician or plumber who are amazing at their work? Or the hairstylist, chef, window washer, car mechanic, and on and on.

Do you cut your own hair? Fix your car? Know how to wire an outlet, fan, or hang a chandelier? No, we call in the expert to help us with the things we admit we can't or don't want to do. Trust me, if you think rehabbing a room in your home is going to be easy and you'll get it done in a few days, then you've never done rehab before. I've thought long and hard about how I could take down the tree in my backyard, without doing too much damage or hurting myself, to save $3,500. Fear of doing damage or hurting myself wins out.

And while I believe we each have a gift, the point here is that we aren't great at most things and we all could use a little help. If you really think about it, you can't do anything without the help of others. I may be writing this book by myself, but I couldn't do it without a pencil and paper or a computer that I certainly do not lay claim to inventing.

What I'm saying is, it's not only okay to seek professional help but smart too. Oh wait, I thought it was taboo to talk about money with others. I don't want anyone to know how bad I am with money or that I don't really know anything about it. Who likes to talk about things they know little to nothing about? Proof you need to seek help from an expert! And like any other career, there are always good people and some not so good people. And since you know so little about investing, insurance, portfolios, and such, how do you find those elusive good ones?

Do not announce to the world you are looking for an advisor unless you enjoy swatting at a wasp's nest while hoping they won't sting you. Look, the deeper your desire to learn more about money, the more effort that is required on your part. Sure, reading this book is a great start, in my opinion, but here's where you need to make an effort and do your homework: You can ask a friend you feel is very responsible with their money if they have an advisor. And if they do, are they happy with the results? If you get positive answers, then you may ask to be introduced to that person. Asking a local chamber is also an effective way to learn about who is committed to the community in that field. Research online, network with others, meet advisors, and see if you feel there is a fit. Trust me, if you don't feel there's a fit, run away. The advisor is doing the same thing—if they are any good. An example of a good advisor is when they start with a question like "What are your financial goals, and what have you done so far toward them?"

There are advisors that are "captive," meaning they work with one company and only provide services and products that company offers. Then there are independent advisors who have a greater range of services and products because they aren't tied to one company. There are pros and cons to each type, but I prefer the independent type as they can look for the best services and products currently available market wide, and that changes often. (Hint: This works well with homeowner's and car insurance in my opinion.) Once you've found a person you believe is a good fit, it's time to start the conversation about what you're looking for and where you're at now with family, money, and/or investments. If the advisor goes right into the services and products they think would be perfect for you without learning of your situation and goals, it's not a good sign and time to continue your search.

You hear things like "We're fiduciary." That person is telling you they're an advisor that is required to act (by law) in your best interest with a duty to preserve good faith and trust. It's a level of ethical standards that they are held to when working with clients. Or maybe you see capital letters after their name on a business card. Those are earned, but it doesn't translate into all-knowing of a subject. It means that person fulfilled the requirements to be able to put those initials on their cards based on the agencies that determine the level they believe provides adequate knowledge to be considered a specialist. Did you follow that?

I love this one: "We only make more money when our clients make more money." The very first question that should come to mind is "How does that work?" The answer is rather simple. They charge a fee that is a percentage of assets under management (known as AUMs in the business). Let's say the fee is 1 percent and you have $100,000 with the advisor. You're paying $1,000 per year for their work. If that person then makes you $50,000 that year, you pay $1,500. If you lose $50,000, you still pay $500.

Other advisors get paid a commission on the service or product they sell. It may be a one-time payment, or there may be residual payments for certain products, like life insurance. How much they get paid and how they get paid is important. And while there are many investments that don't charge a fee or create an out-of-pocket expense, trust me, nothing's free. I recall being asked to sell an annuity to a client for a considerable sum, and I knew it would be a large commission for me that came from the annuity company and not out of the pocket of the client. Large being around $20,000, and that is enough to make a person really want to sell you that annuity. But I first needed to make sure the client understood what an annuity is, ask why they thought it was a promising idea, and what they planned to do with it. I wanted to learn how this investment would fit into the overall plan and make sure they understood how it would affect it, because if they decided later it was a bad idea and wanted out of the investment, there would be a heavy penalty to pay. Never buy into an investment or plan that you don't understand! You need to know what the investment or plan is meant to do (the benefits), how much are you investing, are you comfortable with the amount of investment, and is the risk/reward something you're comfortable with. And when discussing annuities, you better know the difference between guaranteed and hypothetical. I had a friend who wanted a big annuity, and I showed him what I thought was the best one on the market at the time. He liked one from his current advisor as it stated it would provide $100 more a month income than the one I showed him. Mine was guaranteed while the other was hypothetical, and based on the market going forward, equaling the best five years in the history of the market. I told him that if the market were to do that well, then the one I showed him would grow and provide a greater payout when the time came, and I showed him how that would work. I also told him that if the market was going to equal the best five years in its history going forward, why not just put your money there? He then asked if I could sell him the other agent's annuity. I told him I could, but if he wanted that one, to buy it from that agent. I wanted no part of selling something I knew wasn't going to do what he was told it would, and I don't steal another's idea. It was purely hypothetical and based on very poor information, in my opinion. I tried on five separate occasions to get my friend to understand the difference between guaranteed and hypothetical to no avail. I then mentioned he would need a new advisor in a few years (because this investment wasn't going to work), and to lose my number. I wanted no part in working with someone so determined in making a bad decision.

CONCLUSION

Setting financial goals is a dynamic process that requires careful planning, consistent effort, and periodic reassessment. By following these steps, you can build a solid financial foundation and work toward your aspirations. Remember, the key to financial success is staying disciplined, informed, and adaptable to changing circumstances. Pay attention.

And seeking expert advice is not a sign of weakness but a smart decision to improve your financial well-being. No one knows or ever learns everything they need to make the right decision every time in life.

three

The Spending Urge

WE ALL KNOW HOW EASY IT IS TO MAKE PURCHASES BASED on emotion and impulse. Yet, with the right motivation, we can be much more responsible with our spending. Despite this, many of us are driven by an almost instinctual urge to spend our earnings as quickly as we get them. This behavior can be influenced by psychological, cultural, and social factors.

I recall a time when I walked into a store and everything seemed irresistible. I wanted it all, but I was broke and couldn't afford anything. A few weeks later, when I had money to spend, I went back to that store, but nothing seemed quite as appealing, and I walked out empty-handed. That experience taught me the value of slowing down and considering what I truly needed versus what I simply wanted. Just noticing that has changed my perspective on how I shop. I now tend to think longer term with many things I buy. Thoughts like, will I still be wearing this in a year, or will I ever need it again, or what would I gain by having whatever it is I'm considering buying now? Meaning, is it worth buying this now wondering if there's something else I might want that I haven't seen yet, and I won't be able to get if I spend this money now? We can rationalize that we should get it now while we have the money because we may not be able to afford it later. And that kind of thinking is what gets you in trouble. If you don't think you can afford something later, then why are you thinking you can now? The money you spend now is gone forever, so if you think you're going to be short on funds later, then why not hold onto that money now?

PSYCHOLOGICAL FACTORS

Psychologically, our tendency to spend can be boiled down to one simple concept: instant gratification. I want, I want, I want! We crave the excitement of obtaining something new, whether it's a small indulgence like a pack of Oreos or a big-ticket item like a car. This desire often leads us to convince ourselves that we *need* the item immediately, without thinking about the long-term consequences.

Take buying a car, for example. You find the perfect vehicle and decide you must have it as it's so you. In your excitement, you ignore costs like insurance, gas, maintenance, or unexpected expenses like new tires or brakes. Oh, you bought an EV and don't have to worry about gas, huh? You should investigate the cost of installing a charger in your home, as that can cost up to $2,000 or more. And you had better check with your homeowner's insurance folks as they may not allow a charger to be installed inside the garage or attached to the house.

But, what you're typically only thinking about is the monthly payment and negotiating with the salesperson to get a manageable deal. You're not thinking about all the hidden costs—taxes, registration fees, dealership costs, and more that often catch buyers off guard. And let's say that takes you out of your comfort zone on affordability. No problem, instead of a four-year loan, we'll make it a seven-year deal and drop that monthly expense to a level you feel better about financially. Keep in mind that now you're committed to eighty-four monthly payments, not forty-eight. That's eighty-four months of funds you no longer have for anything else. And note that a car typically loses about 50 percent of its value after three years. So, after three years, your car's value is lower than what you owe for it. It's called being underwater, and if you owned property from 2008–2014, you know what I'm talking about.

TIPS FOR SMARTER BUYING

1. **Financing:** Start by consulting your bank about the best way to finance your purchase. Dealerships may offer financing, but it's rarely as good as what you can find on your own. Also, don't trust the credit score you see online; the one used for car loans may differ, and that

will affect the interest rate on the loan, and therefore the monthly payments.

2. **Research:** Take time to research the car's long-term value, reliability, safety, and maintenance costs. If you buy a new model car that just came out on the market, you may have to put up with several recalls. Consider buying a used car as they don't lose as much value when you drive it off the lot. I know, it's hard to pass up that new car smell.

3. **Avoid Impulse Buys:** Resist the urge to rush the process. Salespeople often rely on buyers who are eager to close a deal quickly. I remember in a previous life when I sold cars, our manager would say when a person decides to buy a car, they will do so within forty-eight hours. So, why not be the one who sells it to them?

4. **Don't Reveal Your Budget:** When visiting a dealership, don't answer questions about how much you're willing to spend. Instead, focus on specific cars and negotiate from there. The first question you'll get asked is "What are you looking to spend?" That salesperson will find you a car that costs that much, or maybe a little more. But rarely will it be for less. I remember looking at buying a minivan, and the numbers didn't seem to add up right. I asked the salesperson to show me how they came up with that monthly price, and when he did, I learned all I needed to know and walked out. They had

this little itty-bitty number in the calculation that read something like 0.0016458792 as a cost for financing, and I said I hadn't talked about how I was going to pay for it yet. Turns out, that little number equated to a $100 per month charge, and it didn't matter as they wouldn't take it off the pricing. I was going to have to pay that whether I financed with them or not.

5. **How Do I Know If I'm Getting the Right Pricing?** When purchasing a car, you can calculate what the payments should be simply by dividing the *total* loan and interest amount (that's all the fees and extra's included) by the loan term (number of months). For you mathematicians out there, the formula is:

$$M=P\,[\,i(1+i)^n]\,/\,[(1+i)^n\text{-}1].$$

So, bottom line, when buying a car, do some research on how to finance it and how the car holds up over time with regards to maintenance, safety, and value. Don't rush into the purchase and never state what you're looking to pay. If you say $350 per month, the salesperson will find that car for you. And then add on tax/title/license/doc fees/ etc. that bring the payment up to $400 per month. That person knows from experience that you will find a way to justify the extra $50 per month. New versus used is a personal thing, but beware of a thing called Gap insurance. Gap insurance (the difference between what you owe and what the car is worth) is there to protect the purchase primarily of a new car's value once you drive it off the lot. You've already lost 10 percent at that point and will lose roughly 50 percent in three years. This policy costs roughly $1,000 (it can vary) and is used to protect you from losing too much money should you have an accident and need a new car too soon, as most insurance policies typically only cover current value. Ask your insurance person what your coverage will cost and if this additional gap coverage is necessary *before you buy.*

DELAYED GRATIFICATION

Practicing delayed gratification involves taking time to evaluate your options and making well-considered decisions based on your needs more than your wants. This can help prevent feelings of buyer's remorse that often follow large impulsive purchases.

A friend of mine, a chess master, offered me this advice: "Life is like a game of chess, where every decision affects the outcome. When faced with a decision, pick the best option, and then reassess to ensure it's truly the best move and you haven't missed anything obvious. Only then should you act." Okay, I altered this a tad, but you get the meaning.

SOCIAL AND CULTURAL INFLUENCES

Many of us are driven to spend by social and cultural pressures. We equate success with owning the newest, shiniest things—a big house, a fancy car, or designer clothes. We might say we don't judge others, but we do, and we base it on what we see, not what we know. My father used to say to me, "Believe none of what you hear and only half of what you see." And that has proven true more often than not.

I've seen this play out in many cultures, including my time managing a Japanese brokerage group. In that environment, status was everything, and it was reflected in even the smallest gestures, like how business cards are exchanged.

Social and cultural expectations can push us to spend beyond our means. Maybe you have friends who love to travel or shop at high-end stores, and you feel the need to keep up. But many people who appear wealthy are living paycheck to paycheck or worse. Understanding this can help you make better financial choices. A true friend would never want you to fall into financial ruin just to maintain that friendship. And if they're a really good friend, they may even pay your way.

EMOTIONAL SPENDING

Emotional spending occurs when we buy things to feel better or to reward ourselves. While this can provide a momentary high, it often leads to regret, especially if money was tight to begin with. Whether you're spending to cheer yourself up or to celebrate, it's crucial to recognize these patterns and manage them wisely. Spending money should be fun, and it is when you can afford what you're spending, but it takes a heavy toll when you overspend.

One mindset to try on spending is this: What am I taking away in the future by spending on the now?

POOR MONEY MANAGEMENT: NOT ENTIRELY YOUR FAULT

Poor money management often stems from a lack of education and experience. Schools rarely teach financial literacy, and many people grow up without learning these skills at home. But once you're on your own, the responsibility falls on you to become financially literate. So, as they say in baseball, "Come on, get a glove and get in the game." Money is the one thing that will be with you *forever*, and it will bring with it immense joy and happiness, as well as great sorrow and pain if you're not paying attention.

Want to reduce sorrow and pain, then start saving and investing at an early age. Look, I get that saving money is boring, and investing is slow and confusing if you don't know what you're doing, but if you start at an early age, you will reap greater benefits and enjoy a happier life. I guarantee you will enjoy more of what life has to offer when you're not always worried about money.

THE EMOTIONAL ROLLER COASTER OF BUYING A HOME

Buying a home is often the biggest financial decision of a person's life, and it comes with significant emotional weight. My son and daughter-in-law faced this challenge when their landlord decided to sell the condominium they were renting. With no other affordable options nearby, they had to consider buying, even though they hadn't planned for it. They had been married only a few weeks, and buying a home was not on their radar. On the plus side, they didn't go through many of the emotions that come with making the decision to buy—like finding a realtor, comparing several homes, how many bedrooms and bathrooms, and where the place is located, to name just a few. For them, navigating the process involved understanding property values, finding the right lender to see if they could afford this unexpected purchase, and choosing the best type of loan if they could afford it.

When buying a home, it's easy to get caught up in the excitement and overlook practical considerations, like hidden costs or necessary repairs. A home inspection is vital to avoid costly surprises down the road. Also, don't fall into the trap of stretching your budget for a home that seems perfect but may not be financially sustainable in the long run. It's called being house poor. We typically earn the most income in our lives between the ages of forty-five and fifty-four, so you may be able to buy that home you've always wanted later in life if you plan well.

Another trap when purchasing a home is between the price you say you can afford, and the cost of the house you buy. A realtor will rightly ask you what price range you are comfortable with, and you need to have the discipline of staying within that range. Because what will happen is the realtor will show you a home above your range, and now the homes you look at within your range don't stack up against that more expensive one with all the extras in it. The realtor isn't a bad person for doing this as they are trying to show you the market to set proper expectations. What you need to do is put a check on those emotions so you don't wind up house poor. Ask yourself, what is the purpose of buying this home at this time?

HOME BUYING TIPS

- Start with what you can afford. You'll need to find a lender (bank or mortgage broker are most common) and then choose if you want to get preapproved or prequalified (this means you're serious about buying, both to the realtor and the seller). Preapproved says that, based on a conversation with a lender, they believe you could afford $250,000. Whereas prequalified means that you have gone through a process with the lender and can prove they will provide a loan up to a specific amount. This person will walk you through the loan process, so you want someone you can trust.
- Even if the seller states they are selling "as is," meaning no inspections will be considered in the transaction, and you go through with the purchase, I highly recommend acquiring a home inspection after. It's a small price to pay for a large investment, which could

be much larger if you don't know what to expect. The seller simply doesn't want anyone to find an issue that could drive the price lower or request a concession that reduces their profit. And they easily could be hiding an expensive issue that they're handing off to the next owner.

- Whether you get a home inspection or not, you need to pay attention when looking at the home. Outside you may like the curb appeal, but check the roof to see if anything stands out like discoloration from water damage or missing shingles, as these can be extremely expensive. Check the landscaping to see if it is well maintained, because if it's not, that may mean the house hasn't been either. Inside the home it's fine to see how your furniture will fit, but it's more important to see how it has been maintained. Any roofline leaks in any room you walk into? How about water damage in the bathroom(s) or kitchen? How old are the appliances, heating, AC, and overall ventilation system? If there's a basement, look at the walls for any flood lines, and while there ask about the age of the sump pump. These aren't hard for anyone to do, and I could go on, but at this point you can see the value of an inspection.

- Remember, a house is a structure; what you put into it is what makes it a home. And structures need upkeep that cost money and time. Keep in mind, whatever you change in the home has a cost that needs to be considered next to the value you can expect to get out of it when you sell. It doesn't make sense to add a $50,000 kitchen to a home worth $120,000.

- A suggestion would be to keep a logbook of sorts where you log the date and cost of any repair or new appliance. Include where you bought them as well. If you have someone come to work in your home, write down who it was and what work was completed, their contact information, the cost, and how satisfied you were with the work. You may need them again, a neighbor may ask, or you may want to make sure you don't call them again. Making repairs on or in a home can be costly, so you may want to look online how to do it yourself. YouTube has almost any repair you can imagine for you to learn whether or not you feel the repair is within your ability. Keep in mind, you may find more issues when trying to repair the one you know about, especially in older homes.

- As for the loan process, I'll let you learn about that as you go. But safe to say, it will be the most fun you've ever had and will go quickly. Okay, that may not be true, but you'll get through it. You'll need two months' worth of bank statements and paystubs ready to go. *Just don't make any large purchases or open any new credit accounts while in the process.* I have seen many mistakes by borrowers going out to buy furniture, appliances, a new car, or even a new condo for their mom or dad while in the process that led to a decline for the loan. Nada, nothing, no signing up for a card to get a discount. And don't run up the credit cards you do have as your credit report will be looked at several times, including the day before you get approved. Once again, how a credit score is determined when buying a house is different from other types of loans and may not reflect what you see on the reports you look at. Longer-term loans, like a mortgage, will help grow your credit score going forward, but when you sell your home, your score can drop by one hundred points or more because the long-term loan is coming off the credit report. Don't worry as it will bounce back fairly quickly and can be explained if you're looking for new credit.

BREAKING THE CYCLE

Whether our spending is driven by psychological, cultural, or social factors, it often involves emotional or impulsive decisions. You have the power to change your habits. By doing your homework before making big purchases and questioning the need for smaller ones, you're already on your way to financial well-being.

In conclusion, saving may seem dull, and investing might appear complicated, but both are essential to building a secure financial future. Remember, you control how you handle your money—or do you?

Ultimately, the goal is to live with intention, making informed decisions that align with your values and financial goals. You're already learning to be more thoughtful with your money, and that's another step toward financial freedom.

four

Understanding Debt

DEBT IS A COMMON ASPECT OF FINANCIAL LIFE, OFTEN divided into two categories: good debt and bad debt. The distinction depends on how borrowed money is utilized and its impact on your financial health. Do you know anyone over twenty-five who isn't in debt? If you do, you have friends in high places as debt is a reality for most of us, including our own government. However, it's essential to be cautious with debt, as even good debt can quickly turn into bad debt due to poor choices—or sometimes through no fault of your own.

For example, I bought a house in 1994 at a great price in a desirable neighborhood and sold it for a substantial profit in 2005. Feeling confident in my real estate acumen, I reinvested the profit into a new home we built in a new community. What I didn't foresee was the financial meltdown that was about to unfold in many ways. In 2004, I was the first person in the US to engage in both pit trading and electronic trading simultaneously. It was a chaotic time, with twenty-seven people screaming in one earpiece, another person in the other ear, managing trades both in the pit and electronically all while communicating with multiple people on the trading floor by hand.

I was executing trades for the largest trader at the time, and while we made some impressive trades and learned from our mistakes, I didn't realize this marked the beginning of the end for traditional trading pits. Some remain active, but none are close to the 1,500-person Eurodollar pit at the Chicago Mercantile Exchange I had been a part of.

So, I sold my first home for a great profit and invested in a brand-new house with many of the bells and whistles I had dreamed of. About two years later, I found myself out of a career as computers began to take over trading. And we knew what that meant as we had seen how quickly LIFFE (London Exchange) closed its doors. This, combined with the emerging housing bubble that was about to devastate so many, created a perfect storm. Building a new house was the most expensive way to buy, and I did it at the worst possible time. When the housing bubble burst, new constructions like mine saw the steepest decline in value (over 60 percent). My smart real estate investment turned into a financial disaster, and I had to give up my house and relocate my family. Let's call this a blindsided gut punch.

I'm not seeking sympathy—many were caught in this situation and lost their homes too. It was a hard lesson learned as we loved the home we built, but taking away the emotion and giving it up was the best long-term financial decision at the time.

While I still believe that taking on a mortgage can be a good financial move, it's crucial not to overextend yourself.

GOOD DEBT

Good debt is borrowing that serves as an investment in your future. It usually involves something that is likely to increase in value or generate long-term income. It does not include getting a credit card that pays you cash back. Unless you pay that off every month, it's almost never worth it as the interest rate is high.

Student Loans: Most people view education loans as good debt, until they graduate and have to start paying it back. It's generally thought that a college degree or specialized training can significantly increase earning potential over time. And while student loans can be substantial, the return on investment can justify the expense, leading to better-paying jobs and career opportunities. However, this has been a point of contention in many circles as the middle class has a tendency to seek higher education with the belief it will provide greater income. We are seeing trends now that show this is not always the case as there are folks in vocational jobs now earning a very good income, and in many cases more than those with an MBA or PhD just out of school. Not to mention if you have an entrepreneurial mindset, you may be better off hitting the pavement and start building your dream. Keep in mind that continuing education takes time and costs more money, and that leaves less time in your career for earning income and paying those loans back.

According to Consumer Reports, about 45 percent of people who went to college say it wasn't worth it. It makes sense in that, when we look at what school to go to, the cost doesn't come into play until after those acceptance letters start coming in the mail. Then we figure out how to pay for it, and that includes loans that, for many, hold you back starting six months after graduation. Starting adulthood should not come with a huge debt that stops you from starting a retirement plan, a savings account, or having to put off buying your first car or home. I'm just saying that college isn't for everyone, but it can be a good start for others. You need to do your homework (Like how I fit that in again? Homework?) when planning for college as it has such a significant impact going forward.

Certain fields, such as law, healthcare, finance, and business, still require higher education for long-term benefits, though less and less in business. But keep in mind that only around 57 percent of people with a college degree earn more than those without. Therefore, it's important to carefully consider whether the college experience outweighs the value of four years of work experience. And don't get me started on those online colleges. I read that about 80 percent of those who start never finish, but they keep paying for it thinking they'll get back to it soon.

You see, in the US we believe that everyone should attend college, preferably a prestigious one. The pressure in high school is huge as we tend to look down upon those that choose to go to a community college or vocational school. And let's not forget that the high school has a reputation to uphold with the percentage of students that go on to college. While there are benefits to getting into a top school, like specialization in a desired field, you need to be sure of why you chose the school you did. I bet we all know people who earn college degrees and then work in some completely unrelated career.

Something to keep in mind when looking at schools: If you're unable to get into the one you want right away, consider a local community college, and then transfer a year or two later to your original choice. Many students drop out in the first couple of years, leaving spots open for you to get in. Oh, and you save money this way as well.

I remember showing up to college and going to registration to let the school know Bill Haase was on campus and ready to party, uh I mean, kick ass in class. The folks behind the table looked at me and asked what my major was, and I hadn't ever given it a thought. I responded, "What difference does it make as the first two years are general requirements anyway." I was off to a great start. What never came to mind was if the school would have anything I might want to base a career on. My school choice was based on location and cost from my parents and had nothing to do with what I wanted. To be fair, I had no idea what I wanted and was never known to be a good student (understatement here), but there was never a thought to doing anything else but go to college. That was just the next natural step one took in life from the social position I came from. Later in life I learned there are many kinds of smart, and having a college education doesn't always translate into smart.

While I envy those who knew what they wanted to do for a career at an early age, so few of us have a clue as to what we want to be when we grow up, and we have so little experience and knowledge at a time when we need to make this *huge* decision. Mom and Dad have tried to shelter us from all that life brings to the playing field, and then all of a sudden, our junior or senior year in high school, we must decide what we want to be/do and where is the best college to go to in order to earn the most money when you get out. Ahhhhhhhhh, how do I make that decision? I mean, how many parents ask their child if they would rather go to a vocational school, or if they feel as if they may be more entrepreneurial-minded, or maybe the military is an option. Those college funds you have stuffed away may help your child start a business that will teach them more in four years than most colleges will. But if college is the way forward, you really need to start thinking about it in the seventh and eighth grades so you can determine what courses to take in high school that will help you get into a better college that has what you're looking to do.

Take my friend Jayson I had the privilege of interviewing on my radio show. I met him when he was thirteen or fourteen at an event in Dallas. First, I was already jealous because he was a speaker at the event, and I was not. Why was he speaking? Because he was fourteen and already on his third business. In my interview I learned he had started each business to earn the money to get to the next one. He was now a week or so away from the ripe old age of fifteen, and he had a business with over 300 clients! Great young man with awesome parents, and he was going to an online Christian school for part of his day while doing business the other parts. He had employees (that he had interviewed and negotiated hiring) and was set to buy a truck for his business. He had all the financing figured out, and at age fifteen, he was going to get his learner's permit and a truck. He was also going to hire a twenty-one-year-old because, in the state he lives, an adult was required to sit in your vehicle for you to legally drive on a permit. I have never met a more entrepreneurial-minded person in my life, and he is fortunate to have amazing parents that not only see it but help develop it. Jayson goes to his folks with ideas, and they don't give answers, they ask questions and let him know he needs to convince them why his idea is so good and how it will work. I asked him how he came to make important decisions like hiring someone or buying a truck, and he said in part he prays on it. I'd love to order one hundred Jaysons right now for future ventures to put him in charge of.

Deciding what you want to be when you grow up is challenging. Parents often encourage college without considering other paths like vocational schools, military, or entrepreneurship. Bottom line, there's no perfect path for most of us, and we should help young individuals start thinking about this earlier in life. I know way too many people that are not happy in their work but are tied to the job because of money. They may get paid too much, are afraid to make a change, too deep in debt, or they think they only have another five to ten years before retirement kicks in. We all make excuses, as few of us embrace change, and that's a form of living as a financial hostage. Money controlling you.

Mortgages: Another common example of good debt is a mortgage. Real estate typically appreciates over time, and owning a home can be more cost-effective than renting in the long term. Additionally, mortgage interest is often tax-deductible, reducing the overall cost of borrowing. However, some argue that renting is better since it avoids maintenance costs and unexpected expenses. But renting doesn't allow you to build equity, which can be a significant advantage later in life.

Investment properties are also considered good debt when done properly. These are purchased with the expectation of generating rental income and/or appreciation in value. Investing in real estate can provide tax benefits and diversify your investment portfolio. For instance, a friend of mine "sells dirt"—he buys land ahead of growth trends and profits from its appreciation. The key is to do thorough research and ensure you're not overextending yourself financially.

Business Loans: Borrowing to start or expand a business can also be good debt if managed wisely. Business loans can help generate income and increase your net worth over time. However, many business owners lack a formal plan or understanding of their financials, which can lead to problems. Hiring someone to manage your books is common, but you must have safeguards in place to prevent theft. Several business owners I know discovered too late that trusted employees or family members had stolen significant amounts of money. As mentioned, most small business owners never develop a business plan, and few ever learn about the numbers that go into the books. Sure, they know where each year started, what they spent, and what they brought in money-wise—thus knowing if they're in the black (good) or the red (bad) at the end of the year. But they have no idea where the money is tied up with regards to assets, receivables (they learn about receivables when the money gets tight), and many other areas. And this makes sense in that we can simply hire others to do that work and not have to deal with learning about things you don't already know about. I mean, I have a business to run and don't have time to learn a whole new side of it, right? Fair enough, but remember this, when you hire someone else to do your books, you had better have a fail-safe way to make sure they can't steal from you. If it's easy, someone is going to take it.

In summary, good debt typically involves:
- An asset that appreciates over time (e.g., property, education, business)
- The potential to generate income or improve earning opportunities

- Possible tax benefits
- Debt that is manageable within your budget and not straining your finances

BAD DEBT

Bad debt is borrowing used to purchase depreciating assets or to finance things that do not generate income or increase in value. This type of debt can be detrimental to your financial health, especially if it accumulates over time.

Credit Card Debt

- **Purpose:** Used for everyday expenses, consumer goods, or luxury items.
- **Why It's Bad:** Credit cards often carry high interest rates, and if you don't pay off the balance in full each month, the debt can quickly spiral out of control. Using credit cards to purchase items that depreciate, like electronics or clothing, means you're paying interest on things that lose value quickly. Just listen to those people on TV that rant about how they ran up their credit cards so high it would take fifty-nine years to pay back if they only made the minimum payment. Don't get me started here.

There are many types of credit cards, each suited for different purposes and credit profiles. Reward cards are popular, allowing users to earn cash back, points, or miles on purchases. However, to truly benefit, you must pay off your balance each month to avoid interest charges. Low interest rate cards, balance transfer cards, and co-branded cards all offer different benefits but come with their own risks if not managed carefully.

Characteristics of Bad Debt

- Tied to a depreciating asset (e.g., cars, electronics)
- Does not generate income or improve financial position
- Carries high interest rates
- Often used for nonessential, impulsive purchases

It's highly likely that most, if not all, of you reading this book are carrying some form of debt. The important thing to understand is your spending habits, because if you don't or don't care, you will find yourself on that TV commercial stating you owe over $50,000, and it will take you one hundred years to pay it off. Okay, I exaggerate a bit, but you will find life isn't much fun when you have more debt than you can handle.

Question: How often are the arguments you have with your spouse, children, business partner, or even yourself centered around money? That may be a sign you've taken on too much debt. A key to being able to sleep at night is to be honest with everyone in your life, especially your spouse. Don't hide financial concerns in hopes things will get better like a gambler trying to finally break that bad streak—same with traders. It can easily spiral out of control.

CONCLUSION

Understanding the difference between good and bad debt is crucial for making sound financial decisions. Good debt can help you build wealth and secure your financial future, while bad debt can lead to financial hardship and stress. By focusing on reducing bad debt and using good debt strategically, you can take control of your finances and work toward long-term financial stability.

five

Understanding Credit Scores and How to Build Credit

YOUR CREDIT SCORE, SPECIFICALLY YOUR FICO (FAIR ISAAC Corporation) score, can vary depending on the type of credit you're applying for, whether it's a home loan, a car loan, a major credit card, or a smaller store card. Each type of credit uses a different calculation, so the score the bank tells you might not always be the most relevant one. Rather than getting too deep into the specifics of each calculation, it's enough to know that the lower your credit score, the higher the interest rate you're likely to face. And let's just say that this may be to the lender's advantage in how they calculate your score.

WHAT'S THE DIFFERENCE BETWEEN A CREDIT SCORE AND A FICO SCORE?

A credit score is a three-digit number that reflects your financial health and your ability to manage credit and debt. A FICO score is a specific type of credit score used by lenders to make lending decisions, with each institution making slight adjustments to the calculation. While the FICO scoring system is the most widely used, all credit scores measure the same thing: how likely you are to pay the loan back.

Credit scores range from 300 to 850, with 800–850 considered excellent, 740–799 very good, 670–739 good, 580–669 fair, and 300–579 poor. In 2023, the average FICO score reached 715. However, as credit card debt has surged to an all-time high, more people are spending money they don't have, which suggests potential financial trouble ahead. Studies show that up to 80 percent of our spending is driven by emotion or impulse, which is why it's crucial to understand the reasons for your spending habits. Whether it's a desire for new gadgets, a car, clothing, or necessary expenses like food and housing, identifying triggers can help you take control of your finances.

If you want to take control of your money (and life) you must be on constant guard from all those who wish to separate you from it. How many times a day do you get hit with an email, on social media, a commercial on TV, or a phone call? All offer great deals on services and products they know you want, and eventually you may even give in and buy. We have been trained to be consumers here in the US, and we're incredibly good at it. We've also been subjected to highly emotional visions that pull at our heartstrings to provide money in support of a horrible situation. Think about those poor dogs all chained up and living in terrible conditions. Ever wonder why all these charities only ask for $19 per month? Well yes, most people can afford that small amount, but the real reason is because charities are required to provide a receipt for annual contributions over $250 per the IRS, and that costs money to provide. At $19 per month, you are paying out $228 per year, which you can still write off on your taxes. But be prepared to show proof, like a bank or credit card statement, should you ever get audited.

HOW DOES YOUR CREDIT CARD BALANCE AFFECT YOUR CREDIT SCORE?

The amount of debt you owe on your credit card significantly impacts your credit score. It's not advisable to max out your credit cards because using your entire credit limit can lower your score. A good rule of thumb is to keep your balance below 30 percent of your available credit limit. Some experts even suggest staying under 10 percent for an excellent score. So now, if you're thinking that you just apply for more credit cards and keep each one at that 30 percent level or lower, read on.

DOES THE NUMBER OF CREDIT CARDS AFFECT YOUR CREDIT SCORE?

Yes, the number of credit cards you have will impact your credit score. Having multiple credit cards can lower your debt-to-credit ratio thus improving your credit utilization rate—the amount of credit you use relative to the total credit available. Either way, the amount used will be taken into account for many types of loans or forms of credit and used to determine what's called DTI, or your debt-to-income ratio (a biggie when looking to buy a home). Let's say you have four credit cards that allow you to use up to $3,000 each, but you've only used $1,000 on each for a total of $4,000 accumulated debt, and you're looking to buy a home. The lender will consider the money you have borrowed and owe back ($4,000 because you have a monthly payment to make on that as part of your DTI) AND the amount you have available that you can still borrow after your loan has closed, which in this case would be another $8,000. Another reason not to open a new account at every little shop just to get that 10–20 percent one-time discount.

SHOULD YOU PAY OFF YOUR CREDIT CARD IN FULL OR LEAVE A SMALL BALANCE?

It's generally a good idea to pay off your credit card balance in full whenever possible. Carrying a balance incurs interest charges and raises your credit utilization rate, which can negatively impact your credit score. There's no meaningful benefit to carrying a small balance on your credit card.

DOES PAYING OFF A MORTGAGE LOWER YOUR CREDIT SCORE?

Many people worry that paying off a mortgage will lower their credit score, and this can sometimes be true. According to credit experts, including my friend known as the Credit Genius, your score might take a temporary dip when you pay off a significant long-term debt like a mortgage. This is because a mortgage is a substantial factor in determining your creditworthiness because it's the longest-term loan you have, and its removal can affect the lender's assessment of your financial stability. However, this dip is usually short-lived, and your score should rebound over time.

I'm not going to go any deeper into the weeds regarding credit scores, as we all know when we're in over our heads with debt and that it has a negative effect on our ability to acquire new money via loans or other forms of credit—not to mention sleep, productivity, and attitude. Besides, it would take another book, or several, to cover everything. I can let you know that the current processes to determine scores used today are not the most efficient ones available and are quite antiquated. Let's just say that lenders like to go with what they know, and I have no interest in pissing them off.

If you wish to dive deeper into the credit score world just look up my friend at http://creditgeni.us.

HOW TO IMPROVE YOUR CREDIT SCORE (AND DO IT FAST)

The most obvious way to improve your credit score is to pay off your debt, but that isn't always feasible. Here are some other basic strategies:

- **Make Timely Payments:** Consistently pay your bills on time.
- **Pay Down Revolving Debt:** Focus on reducing balances on your credit cards.
- **Don't Close Your Oldest Accounts:** These contribute positively to your credit history.
- **Avoid Opening New Credit Accounts:** Resist the temptation to open new accounts just for a discount.
- **Check Your Credit Report Regularly:** Ensure it accurately reflects your financial situation and make sure no new accounts were opened without your knowledge.

Let's say you have several cards with high balances, and it's starting to feel like you'll never pay them off. One idea would be to learn if you could get a single loan to cover all the debt. Of course, this only works if the loan's interest rate is lower than the credit card rates. You could go to the bank and inform them of what you're trying to accomplish, and they may help you, but you'll have to close out the credit card(s) that are getting paid off. You could go right back out and get another card or two, but that will only put you into deeper debt. When you pay off and close a credit card, it is heard around the credit world, and many will seek you out with some great offers. You must remain strong!

DEBT CONSOLIDATION AND CREDIT REPAIR SERVICES

You've no doubt heard about the fast-growing industry of debt consolidation, and I've already touched on this subject previously, but it's worth going over again. Here's the thing, you can call the credit companies yourself and see what they are willing to do just like these companies would do. The problem here is that if all your payments have been on time, the credit company is going to want to understand why you're calling to reduce the debt and create a payoff situation, which is typically a life-altering event such as a job loss or divorce. While it is illegal for anyone to tell you that you need to be behind on payments even a month or two in order to provide a better bargaining position, I have no doubt there is a way of making this known when in conversations with these types of entities you see on TV. I don't recommend this course of action as it may remain on your credit report for up to seven years, just like declaring bankruptcy. But if you believe that is your only choice, just make sure you have everything in writing and understand the new payments and time frame to be debt free. If you believe you need to declare bankruptcy, I strongly suggest you speak with a lawyer that specializes in that area, as the debts to be discharged can be determined by what chapter you use. The most common ones are Chapters 7 and 13, as these are for personal bankruptcies, but there are also Chapters 9, 11, 12, and 15.

Keep in mind, lawyers are like doctors in that they typically specialize in certain areas. But I made a huge mistake one day when I went on social media to ask if anyone knew a good contract lawyer. I quickly learned that *all* lawyers do contract work, as that's what they learn in their first semester of law school. Again, if you go this route, get everything in writing and make sure you know what to expect for payments and the date you will be debt free.

I'LL SAY IT AGAIN

For those of you who have the buying of their first home still on the horizon, I want you to know this: As a previous processor and underwriter of real estate loans (residential), once you are in the process of getting a loan with a lender, do *not* open any new lines of credit, no new car, no opening a furniture store account to fill the new home, no buying your mother a condo, no new expensive jewelry, no trip around the world on existing credit cards—nada, nothing that has to do with any major movements of funds or expenditures. It will be used against you, cause the loan process to take longer, and possibly cost you that loan and the new home.

CONCLUSION

Look, credit can be good or bad depending on how you use it and how much. There are many safeguards in place to help you, but there are just as many ways to get yourself into some big trouble that could take years to get over. The point here is to introduce you to the influences of money that you don't typically see or encounter consciously but affect your world every day. I spent sixteen years executing interest rate futures, and what I learned was that interest rates affect everything that has to do with money everywhere in the world. It affects your credit score, ability to buy a home or car, most definitely your credit card rates, travel, and even the cost of the goods you like to buy. It affects what you can and cannot afford, and you need to pay attention to this closely, but not as close as your spending habits and how to control those. If you can't seem to get a grip on your spending habits and develop a good money mindset, please seek out a coach. All you have to do is Google "money coach."

six

Investing

WHAT IS INVESTING IN SIMPLE TERMS?

At its core, investing is like a forced savings plan but with greater potential for growth. People invest for various reasons, usually to meet a future need or goal. You've heard the phrase "Make your money work for you." That's what investing aims to do. A savings account is a safe bet but is limited as to how much you can earn from it and typically falls below the cost-of-living index. Meaning, you lose buying power if the only place you have your funds is in a savings account, whereas an investment can have unlimited upside potential.

Most people understand inflation to some degree—it's the rising cost of goods and services over time, which reduces your purchasing power. For example, if your money is sitting in a savings account earning 1 percent interest while the cost of living rises by 5 percent, you're losing

4 percent in purchasing power that year. Your $100 today will only be worth $96 in a year. So, letting your money sit and decrease in value isn't always the best option; instead, you need to find ways to make it work for you. That's where investing comes in.

Investing is also about taking calculated risks with your money. Many people invest to achieve specific goals, like saving for retirement or buying a house. When considering how to get started investing, it's better to start with the question "What am I investing for?" rather than "What should I invest in?" The reason behind your investment will guide you toward the appropriate options. Most people think investing only involves buying stocks or bonds, but a diversified portfolio can include much more—like real estate, jewelry, coins, gold, and life insurance. A portfolio is a collection of financial investments.

Here's where things can get complicated. You might end up needing a lawyer for a trust, an accountant for taxes, an insurance agent for policies, and another professional for stocks and bonds. The problem is that these professionals often don't communicate with each other, which means your investments might not be working together toward your original goal. You're left managing everything yourself, which can be overwhelming. Make sure all your advisors are aware of what the others are doing to maintain a risk level you're comfortable with, and it remains focused on the why. Many financial advisors can help you with investing and the various life insurance options, but you'll want to ask them how they balance the two toward your goals and needs, as many advisors tend to focus on one or the other and may not be proficient at how the two can make for a stronger and more efficient portfolio.

WHEN SHOULD YOU START INVESTING?

It's never too early to start investing. Some young adults are already experimenting in the market, buying stocks, bonds, or futures, and they're learning valuable lessons early on. But if you're like many people who have just finished college or started a new job or business, you're thinking it's time to start putting money away. That's a smart move—the earlier you start, the better off you'll be when it comes time to retire or sell your business.

One common way to begin is through a 401(k) plan, either offered by your employer or one you've set up yourself through your business. Maybe you already participate in one but have no idea how much of your income you should put into it or what options provided are the best ones for you. To start, one common train of thought is to put in the percentage the company matches, as that would be known as free money (if they match 3 percent then put in 3 percent to get the full benefit being offered). It's an incentive the company will give to support your efforts to save for later in life. Not all companies match what you put in, and others may only match at certain levels. It never hurts to go over the options with a professional so that you understand what to expect. Yes, I know HR is there to help, but nowadays they'll send you to some link in their system that's supposed to explain it to you via video. It may not be so easily understood, and who do you reach out to if you have questions? I've seen so many 401(k)s from other people that are invested in an option that doesn't align with their goals, or simply is growing too slowly and will have to make up ground in the future.

Target-Date Funds are a common investment option for 401(k) accounts. Individuals choose a fund that closely matches their year of retirement, and it will rebalance assets automatically until that target date is reached. An example is if you're thirty years old in 2025 and plan to retire at age sixty, the target date of 2055 would be the proper choice. This option came about in 1994 and was intended to let you "set it and forget it" if you're not sure what to do or not interested in having to watch over it year after year. These funds can be made up of mutual funds alone, or they may include bonds to reduce the risk. Over time, the fund will adjust (rebalance), going from the higher risk mutual funds to the lower risk bonds with the intent to lower your overall market risk as you get closer to retirement. One negative to this option is Target-Date Funds are not individualized for a person's specific situation because they treat every person who will retire in a certain year as the same. However, not every person is the same. They have different income needs, lifestyles, and resources in retirement. People should have an individualized income plan for retirement, and Target-Date Funds can't do that.

Remember, it's better to look at investing asking, "What am I investing for?" rather than "What should I invest in?"

And now it gets a little tricky because you may have a choice of this account being an IRA (Individual Retirement Account) or a ROTH IRA, developed in 1998 and named after William J. Roth, a Republican senator from Delaware. It's always nice to have choices. With an IRA, you take a portion of your earnings *before* it gets taxed, place it into the 401(k), and then choose what to invest it in. It's nice because you have now lowered your current income since it's taken out of each paycheck prior to you getting hit with taxes. However, it will be taxed later in life as you go to withdraw it, which shouldn't be until you retire. More on this in a minute.

A ROTH IRA is an individual retirement account that lets you contribute money that has *already* been taxed and allows your investments to grow tax-free. But here's the kicker, when you withdraw the funds in retirement, it's tax-free. So, the question is, do you want to pay taxes now or later? The difference is that you know what the taxes are now, but you have no idea where they'll be when you retire.

I'm afraid to tell you this, but both choices allow you to gain access to the funds through a typically low interest rate loan where you start repaying that loan very quickly through your paycheck (think reduced income). And it's tax-free because it's a loan. I'm afraid to tell you this because too many people take out loans then leave their job/company for whatever reason and close out the account to receive all the funds. When a person does that, they become liable for all the taxes due on the full amount and typically pay an additional fee of about 10 percent. The fee comes out immediately while the taxes due will be at your next filing. I know, you were let go and need the money, but, unless you're in dire straits, it's best not to withdraw these funds if you can help it. Your best option if you leave your job for any reason is to move those funds to an advisor that can set up the proper account so you may continue to contribute at your leisure and not have the burden of taxes due. This is called rolling it over. The nice thing about rolling your account is that you will have many more options to choose from for investing than what a 401(k) provides.

Side Note: There are still some jobs that provide what is known as a pension, but very few people see these anymore. In recent decades, private companies have been moving away from traditional pension plans (also known as *defined benefit plans*) toward defined contribution plans like 401(k)s. Notice the subtle change in words here, defined *benefits* plan versus defined *contribution* plan. Pensions were made up of stocks (which may be that company's stock), bonds, and possibly real estate that the company was responsible for and to your benefit. This required the company to contribute to a pool of funds set aside for a workers' benefit that would pay a guaranteed monthly income in retirement (or they may offer a lump-sum payout), while now the contribution option being offered puts that responsibility onto you, the employee. This shift is due to several factors, including economic strains on companies, changing workforce preferences, and the complexity of managing pensions. 401(k)s are cheaper and put more risk on the employee while offering tax benefits and easier savings through automatic deductions.

By now you may be saying to yourself, "Defined benefits, defined contribution, stocks, bonds, insurance, 401k's, ahhhhhhhhh, it's too much! This is why I don't want to know about money because it's hard to learn, know, and plan for all this." Stay with me here because the truth is there will be a point in your life where you'll come across most if not all of this stuff, and I'm just trying to give you a taste of what to expect. Remember, my mission statement is "I provide knowledge, knowledge gives you options, and options give you freedom."

DIVERSIFY YOUR INVESTMENTS

The thing with 401(k)s is they are limited in options for investing and very few people ever put enough money in to make a meaningful difference for their needs later in life. The smart thing to do is put some in the 401(k) (remember about the company matching) and invest more funds in other ways like an IRA or a ROTH with an advisor. This will provide you with more options, and the more you invest now, the better off you will be in the future.

To build a more substantial financial foundation, consider investing in additional assets beyond your 401(k), IRA, or ROTH. These could include land, rental properties, gold, cryptocurrency, or a business.

Common investment options include stocks, bonds, mutual funds, Exchange-Traded Funds (ETFs), and even life insurance. Here's a quick overview of risk levels from highest to lowest:

- Futures (highest risk)
- Individual stocks
- Stock options
- Mutual funds
- ETFs
- Bonds
- Life insurance
- Savings account, CDs, money markets (lowest risk)

Futures

When trading futures like those of the S&P 500 Index, traders may buy a futures contract, agreeing to purchase shares in the index at a set price months from now or sell the contract before expiration. If the index goes up, the value of the futures contract will increase, and they can sell the contract at a profit before the expiration date. Of course, what goes up can come down, and just as quickly. Do not attempt to trade any futures without proper oversight. My trader friends would laugh at this brief definition (they would say lame), but it's my way of saying, "Don't trade futures." It took me years to understand all the nuances of futures along with needing to learn Deltas and Gammas for rate of changes when doing options on futures. Just go to Vegas and have fun there.

Stocks and Stock Options

Oh boy, how does one inform others about trading stocks? A monkey throwing darts can be as effective as any other idea on some days, comes to mind. But there are ways to trade with calculated risk that you can do on your own through a website, or you can engage a professional to help you make or learn how to make better decisions. You need to determine the level of risk you're comfortable with and go from there. Every advisor is obligated to record risk tolerance when working with you.

Individual stocks may have dividends that will pay you for owning them on a quarterly or annual basis regardless of where the price of the stock has gone while owning it. Truth is, you need to do your homework and learn about trends and charting to see things like momentum (also known as the trend), support, and resistance lines. The trend is every trader's friend, and we follow it until it makes a clear change in direction.

I will say this: If you think you have a "hot" stock tip from a friend of a friend, and it's going to make you rich... you do not have nor ever will have a true "hot" tip, period. If your tip does pay out big, there very easily could be a special eight-by-ten-foot luxury room waiting for you in a very nice correctional center. Do not participate or get involved with insider trading. Think about it, how is it that you have somehow come across this hot tip that so few know about? When we were in the pits, we would explain it away as thinking we are on the inside, and therefore the tip must be good. Looking back, it's laughable how our egos would get in the way of common sense.

The average person will invest over a twenty-to-forty-year period, and it's important to know—and all advisors will tell you—that investing over a longer period of time in the market has proven beneficial. This is based on looking at the DJIA (Dow Jones Industrial Average, made up of the top thirty stocks) over 125+ years where only twice has the market provided a lower return at the end of a ten-year period from where it had begun, during the Great Depression of 1930 and the Great Recession in 2008. Much like owning a home, it has proven to be a safe opportunity to grow your money over time. So, please don't get caught up in the day-to-day DJIA ups and downs.

You need to, once again, do your homework when looking to buy stocks. Don't just listen to those "experts" on TV telling you this or that stock is looking to grow given the current economic environment. There's a reason why a law exists that states a person recommending a stock must inform you if they own it. I can assure you that those experts will talk about the market in a manner that fulfills the support of their position in said market.

Stock Options (each option represents an underlying entity, like a specific stock) allow you to buy or sell the underlying stock in the future at a specific price and by a certain date until the option expires (they are traded quarterly but some can be monthly). There are Call and Put options available. When you buy a Call option, you believe the stock price is going to increase in a certain time limit, and when you buy a Put option, you think the stock will decrease in price over a certain time period. Option values are determined by intrinsic and time components. As you probably suspect, there's a lot more to this type of trading, and you'd be right. But for the purposes of this book, purchasing an option is done because it's less expensive and carries a slightly lower risk than owning the stock outright. A *VERY* basic example is a stock option may cost $10, while the underlying stock is currently trading at $100. If you own the stock and it goes to zero, you'd lose $100, but the option can only lose the $10. There are situations where an option can have unlimited possibilities, so not for the faint of heart. And those who trade options typically also calculate Deltas and Gammas, which detect the rate of change in pricing between the stock and the option. This has to do with the time limit involved with the option expiration date. They can also get very confusing and be used in more ways than I care to explain. Some strategies commonly used are called Strangles, Straddles, Butterflies, and even Iron Butterflies that get extremely confusing. Once again, do not attempt to trade options without proper oversight. Have I scared you away from trading options?

Mutual Funds

Mutual funds let you pool your money with other investors to "mutually" buy stocks, bonds, and other investments. They're run by professional money managers who decide which securities to buy (stocks, bonds, etc.) and when to sell them. You get exposure to all the investments in the fund and any income they generate. They allow investors to dollar-cost average over time (buy into the fund using new money or dividends to average out the overall purchase price) and reinvest dividends enabling compound growth. However, taxes on capital gains distributions and dividends can make them less tax efficient, and there may be penalties for withdrawing early. These typically have a settlement price at the end of each day where a person can buy in or sell.

An Exchange-Traded Fund is a type of fund that can hold many assets, much like a mutual fund, but is traded like an individual stock on an exchange in that it can be bought or sold at any time during trading hours. It's important to understand that investing in mutual funds or ETFs still involves risk as your money is fully invested in the market, but it is considered a lower risk option to individual stocks.

Bonds

A bond is simply a loan taken out by an entity, like a company or a government. Instead of going to a bank for a loan, the company gets the money from investors who buy its bonds. In exchange for the capital, the entity pays interest, typically on an annual basis. There are many strategies involved with owning bonds, but the important thing to know here is that they are considered a lower risk investment. Notice I didn't say no risk? Recently, our interest rates increased, and that means those who issue bonds need to increase the rate they offer. Note that when this happens, the lower interest rated bonds you bought five years ago tend to lose value in the market quickly, as there are higher interest rate bonds now available and thus more desirable. What would you rather own, a bond that pays 3 percent annually, or one that pays you 7 percent? And the folks issuing the higher interest rate bonds take on greater risk as they have to pay it back, leaving less for them. The typical bonds most people look into are US government, municipal, and corporate. So not 100 percent risk free.

Life Insurance
Ah, last but not least, and not as boring as you've been led to believe: *Life insurance*. It's the one investment that can grow at a decent rate and with almost zero risk. For the sake of this book, I'll try to limit the many wonderful things a policy can do for you and keep it simple, somewhat. The two types of policies most people have heard of are Term and Whole Life, and they are used for different purposes. A term policy is the least expensive and most popular (accounting for about 84 percent of all policies) because it's cheap, covers you for a set number of years, has no tax restrictions or rules, and is easy to use. A suitable time to buy some Term insurance is when you're buying your first home to help cover the mortgage, should something happen to the bread winner in the family, especially if the bread winner is also a business owner. I've seen and heard horror stories of the bread winner passing away for whatever reason and the spouse and children are left

with no viable business and no way to pay the mortgage. There are other reasons a Term policy may be just what you need, but one argument I don't like when deciding between Term and Whole Life is that it's cheaper when you're younger. Insurance of any kind is always less expensive when you're younger, but that doesn't mean it's the right one. Whole life is an investment of different proportions as it grows in cash value over time (Term has no cash value as it's more like leasing a car), and that cash value may come in handy later in life when you do want to buy a home or for some other financial need. I know people who use their policy much like a bank. They borrow from it at a lower interest rate than the market bares and pay themselves back with interest (so it grows faster) with the option of skipping a payment (or all the payments) if they want to. It's your money and the worst that can happen is the benefit is reduced by the amount that is owed from the loan upon payout. The growth rate varies depending on several factors, so check with an agent to learn the current market expectations. I sure wish I had purchased a Whole Life policy when I was young. It costs more, but the benefits far outweigh a Term policy. While there are many types of life insurance, the only other one I'll bring up is LTC (Long Term Care). I was a CLTC (Certified Long-Term Care) specialist, and I understand the real value of this type of policy since I have the initials, lol. Remember earlier in the book I mentioned about folks who had those initials after their names on business cards. Well, these were my initials: CLTC. And I would liken it to taking an ice tray, filling it with water, putting it in the freezer, and coming back three to four hours later (the time I put in to earning the initials), and you have ice. You may now call yourself an ice expert and place the initials ICE after your name on your business card. But, this is an insurance policy that will help pay the bills later in life when we find ourselves needing healthcare that's hard to afford. Healthcare is a cost that has rarely ever seen pricing go down, and I'm quite sure we're all going to run into health issues at some point. There are some amazing types of LTC products out there, and you really need to speak with an agent to learn which ones work best for your needs. Some grow in cash value you can use later or help continue to pay for the policy and include a death benefit. A good LTC policy will guarantee your money back in some form: take back the payments you've made, grow in cash you can use as you wish, pay for medical bills, and have a death benefit. Oh, and you and your spouse can be on a single policy that will pay for each of you should/when you need it. Even if both of you need it at the same time.

Okay that was a bit more than I wanted to say, but I honestly love insurance for the financial stability it can provide at the lowest risk for investing. You should have some in your portfolio, and remember to only purchase a policy from a highly rated insurance company. Notice I mentioned lowest risk, and not zero risk. There have been companies that have gone out of business for not allocating funds properly, but it's exceedingly rare. Now, let's get back to risk...

A WORD ON MARKET RISKS

The stock market has inherent risks, and while mutual funds or ETFs may help mitigate some of them, they won't necessarily move in tandem with major market indicators like the Dow Jones Industrial Average (DJIA). The DJIA is often mentioned in the news, but it only represents thirty large companies, whereas there are thousands of publicly traded stocks. And the movements of the DJIA may not reflect what's happening with your specific investments. You will hear advisors tell of how the market (DJIA) was up 20 percent for the year, and you wonder why your investments only went up 7 percent. You would have had to buy the thirty DJIA stocks at the opening of the first trading day of the year and sell them at the end of the last trading day of the year in order to equal the gains that are stated annually. Most people typically would not own the top thirty stocks at the same time. You may have owned some or all of the same stocks within a mutual fund you had invested in, but you had other stocks that did not perform as well.

I know all about risk as I was part of a handful of people in an office doing risk arbitrage on October 19, 1987, which remains the largest one-day market decline in history. You may think 508 points down isn't that bad, but it was called Black Monday, and those 508 points equaled 22.6 percent of the total market value lost in one day. Risk arbitrage, at the time, was buying or selling large baskets of stock while doing the opposite in the futures market that represented those stocks (think top 500 stocks versus the S&P 500 Futures). We would sell a basket of up to 500 different stocks worth somewhere between $12–$15 million each and purchase the S&P 500 Futures against it. Over and over and over. Okay, I'm getting a bit too deep here, and I'm not trying to scare you about investing in the markets. There are plenty of low-risk options, and I go back to saying how valuable it is to work with a professional. Besides, they stopped doing this particular trading many years ago.

HOW MUCH SHOULD YOU BE SAVING AND INVESTING?

Many financial experts recommend saving 10–15 percent of your income each year. If you're putting 3 percent into a 401(k) and getting a company match of 3 percent, you're effectively at 6 percent, but you should aim to save an additional 4–9 percent in other investment vehicles. Your specific strategy will depend on factors like your age, how much you're investing, your investment performance, how much time you have until retirement, and what you're looking to accomplish. Remember what you're investing for? I've failed to mention the most basic investments available, those being Certificates of Deposit (or CDs) and Money Markets. These are short term and low rate return options for those who don't like higher risk and want better than savings account returns. But keep in mind, there is a penalty for taking the cash out before the term ends, so make sure you do not foresee a need for those funds until after the term ends when purchasing these products.

It's also wise to reduce your investment risk as you get closer to retirement. This strategy helps protect your assets against significant market downturns that could derail your plans. *The most vulnerable time when investing is the five years before and after retiring.* Keep in mind that investing is a long-term game, often spanning twenty to forty years. Daily market fluctuations, or even occasional crashes (some like to call these days a market correction), shouldn't cause panic; over time, your money will grow.

UNDERSTANDING MARKET TRENDS

What's interesting to me is how those in the financial advisement world are not allowed, by law, to use the history of the market to provide insight as to what to expect in the future. Yet every business does just that every year all over the world. I mean, why wouldn't you look back at how the market has been affected when similar situations have occurred over the years to gain an idea of what you can expect going forward? Okay, looking back doesn't clearly provide one with any true indication of what to expect going forward because the market will do whatever it will do. But I know traders remember history, and some can see when it's about to repeat itself. And traders also go by the theory "The trend is your friend!" so when a market consistently moves in one direction, you go with the flow.

Trying to pick a change in direction is tricky at best, much like trying to pick the top or bottom of a stock or index movement. You're best off not trying that as one of two things will happen: You either pick wrong and get hurt, or you pick correctly and think you're all-knowing about the market. That will cost you later, I promise. One thing I have noted over the years is that the market has a tendency to trade in the direction that creates the greatest amount of pain. That is, when the majority of professionals believe the market is heading in a particular direction, it tends to go the opposite way. I think it does that just to piss the professionals off and let them know they don't control it.

ENOUGH ABOUT INVESTING

I just received an email with the subject line: "You've wanted something new. Now's the time to get it." It offered instant financing for a purchase, encouraging me to buy something I want and they have without taking any money out of my pocket. This highlights why I'm writing this book—not to teach you everything about investing, but to help you understand your relationship with money and how to gain control over it.

Managing your money and investing wisely are critical steps toward financial freedom. Keep learning, keep planning, and remember, every decision you make today will impact your future financial well-being.

seven

Let's Have Some Fun.
What They Don't Tell You

THE GOAL OF ADVERTISING IS SIMPLE: TO GET US TO BUY something regardless of where you stand financially. No one cares if you must go into debt to purchase their product or services, and the tactics they use work. You need this or you want that, or they even tell you who you are and what you should be. It's called Shaming! They'll use certain celebrities and athletes and tell us if we buy and use their product, we'll look and feel like that beautiful person you see on the screen. Ever see a commercial for a new car sitting in a trailer park? No, because if we buy that car, it won't represent us as we'd like to be seen. But take that car and put it in front of a gorgeous house on a mountainside with a beautiful spouse and children, snow falling, add a bow as a Christmas gift, and you've got the makings of a lifestyle most of us would love to enjoy. Christmas is the easiest time of year to sell, and the hardest time for us to rein in our spending, because when we're feeling good and "in the spirit of giving," we spend more freely.

There are several agencies that make and enforce the rules for advertising, like the FTC, FDA, CFPB, and the EPA. The rules they've made include:

- Advertisers must be truthful and not misleading
- Advertisers must have evidence to back up claims
- They cannot be unfair about the benefits or attributes of the product or service

Took me a while to stop laughing as well. Those rules alone would make you think that everything that is said about a product or service in advertising is the truth. So, they say little about the product and go straight to using persuasive techniques to lure you in. They appeal to your emotion, use peer pressure, social media, and repetition to convince you. There are three persuasive methods used to get to you: Ethos, Pathos and Logos.

Ethos involves endorsing a product with likeable celebrities or respected experts. Pathos is the use of emotional experiences to connect with, while Logos is the use of facts or data. Then there's comedy that comes into play. Think of commercials with special lines that made us laugh like "Where's the beef?" That line wasn't written into the script, but when a little old lady asked it while recording, it was an instant hit, and she became famous. And hey, who doesn't love watching the Super Bowl for the commercials? Those can cost a lot of money. In the first Super Bowl the cost was

$37,000, and in 2021 the cost rose to $16.8 million. But we never think about how many products need to be sold to pay for that, or how that drives up the cost of the product. There are companies that don't advertise for the sake of keeping prices down, but I would never accuse the health industry of lacking in advertising, with it being divided into two sections called supplemental and drug, and the rules are vastly different for each.

There are those supplements that claim to help with memory. They have no real proof. One of them I know of was originally a dietary supplement that failed miserably, so they pulled it off the shelf, renamed it, and said it helps prevent memory loss. Bingo! Sales went way up. But it doesn't treat or prevent memory-related health conditions like Alzheimer's at all, as the company study showed it was no more effective than a placebo. This stuff doesn't come cheap either, with pricing ranging from forty to sixty dollars per month, as you can choose from the regular or extra strength. Is there a difference in results from one to the other? We may never know, but they'll sell it making you think or feel that extra strength must be better. We've already been trained on that front, and we seem to be fine with taking supplemental pills even when we have no idea what's in them.

It's important to know that supplements are not treated like drugs with the FDA. They don't go through rigorous tests to make sure they do what they say they do and with what side effects. Drugs are tested using clinical trials before being released to the public and are continually regulated. Supplements are primarily thought of as extensions of dietary products, not tested and not regulated.

And yet we see it all the time where outrageous claims are made by using what is known as Puffery. Some examples are "World's best coffee" (how do you prove that?), "Bigger bag means greater value" (only if it contains more goods at the same price), and—here's one you might remember from the '90s— "Better ingredients, better pizza." Puffery is the making of a claim so outrageous that nobody would believe it, but some of us do, and that's why it's used.

In whatever way, when people are trying to sell us, they typically only discuss the benefits. This is an old and frequently used tactic in sales. Tell us how we benefit from using your product and leave out the negatives. Just try to listen to the side effects of any new drug that comes out. And to cover their butts, they tell you that all the side effects can be found in a magazine in the form of yet another ad.

Think about that. They know we don't do our homework on what we buy, or even put in our bodies. Take JUUL, for instance, a vapor substitute for cigarettes. The idea was sold as a healthy way to quit smoking real cigarettes. The only problem was, it proved to be a very unhealthy product. Young adults to middle-aged folks were winding up in the hospital with the need to be induced into a coma to get past the effects and regain their health.

Have you ever watched a commercial and thought, "Yes, that's exactly what I need," then rushed to buy it? I hope not, because most marketing campaigns leave out something that might change your mind about the product. They assume we're not smart enough to notice.

Take those life insurance ads, for example. They say if you're between fifty and eighty-five years old, you can't be turned down, regardless of health, and it costs just $9.95 a month for everyone. Sounds great, right? But they don't tell you for how long you'll be paying that $9.95. More importantly, they don't tell you the payout benefit or how long you must pay before the policy will pay out the full benefit. It could be just a few hundred dollars to a couple of thousand with a two-or-more-year waiting period to reach full death benefit. And after years of payments, you may wind up paying more than what the policy gives back— potentially creating tax issues and penalties. My research showed that, for a sixty-eight-year-old, $9.95 gets you a death benefit of $762 for a male and $1,112 for a female. And an eighty-year-old male would receive $426 while a female would get $608. Doesn't sound like a particularly worthwhile investment to me, but you decide.

I love the commercial where a nice person with big puppy eyes looks into the camera and says, "We know these are challenging times, and if you're thinking about those cheapo life policies you've seen on TV (and yet this commercial is on TV), we've got a solution for you. For the same pricing we can get you more benefit." They don't really care about how challenging the times are for you, they just want to get your money. Now you've got me started. I love the one that asks if you know about the 3 Ps. A price you can afford, a price that will never change (this is a good thing), and a price that's within your budget. And I'm sitting in my chair screaming, "If I can afford the damn price, then it must be within my budget!" But then I realize that they're not marketing to people like me. Though it still upsets me because they're going after folks who could do better with that money.

Again, what about car commercials? They show people racing through a city, over a mountain top, or up a steep hill, but how many of us drive that way? If you did, you'd likely wreck your car or lose your license. But if I buy this car, I'll identify with that type of person. No, you won't—unless you drive around in a minivan. With a minivan everyone looks like a family person. I was once told it's impossible to look cool in a minivan.

Sales tactics are wide ranging, and we've been pro-grammed to fall for them. Ever seen a carpet store without a sale sign in the window? Or gotten a coupon in the mail? Think about this, those mailer coupons get opened only 3–5 percent of the time, as the rest go straight to the gar-bage can, and yet we still get them every week. How can a 3 percent chance to sell your product be cost-effective? But they come every week, which means they work—for some.

Coupons aren't there to help you save money; they're there to get you in the store so you spend more. Sure, you might save a few dollars, but how much did you spend to get that savings? Have you ever walked out of a sale with more money than when you walked in? Bottom line, the word "sale" triggers something in us, and we love to get a discount on anything. You may save $100 on a pair of shoes, but you still spent $300. How are you better off, as that's money you'll never see again? Oh right, you get a cool pair of shoes you've always wanted that will end up in the bottom of a pile of shoes in six months to a year.

Stores are clever too. They'll offer you a discount if you sign up for their credit card. Yay, 20 percent off today! But now you have another credit card on your report, which could cause problems later. And let's be honest, you have enough clothes in your closet already, but fashion trends and seasons keep us coming back for more. Last year's fall color was one shade, this year it's another, and suddenly you "need" new clothes. And if I sign up for that new card, I can buy more things and just charge it.

Apps are another relatively new phenomenon, especially in the fast-food market. The point of having you sign up for an app is not to give you a super discount, as that's the lure. It's to get your information so they can then advertise directly to you whenever they want. Oh, and then they'll sell your information for more income.

And don't get me started on rebates. Broadly speaking, a rebate is a sum of money that is credited or returned to a customer on completion of a transaction. The reality is most of us think a rebate is cash back, and that makes us vulnerable. There's a certain home improvement store that claims you will get an X percent rebate for most purchases, and then they tell you it's a discount on your next in-store purchase. So, you don't get any money back on that first purchase (or ever), but you will get credit if you return to the store and spend more money. Brilliant, just keep going back and spending more of your money. Oh, and you must go through some effort and do so in a specific way, or you don't get that "rebate." They count on many of us being lazy and not willing to go through the required effort and/or do so properly, and they're right as many don't.

I enjoy watching commercials—not for what they're selling, but for how they go about it. There's always something left out, some piece of information that may discourage you from buying that product or service. Like those folks who claim they can protect you from others stealing your information and money. They forget to mention that when monitoring a credit report, they can only see what has been reported. Now, how many people stealing like to report that they're stealing? A bank account or investment account can be opened without anyone ever knowing who opened them as it's all done online. And if it's a credit card, that may not be used and reported for 60+ days. That's a long time before anyone has a clue they've been compromised, and the damage is done.

And what about those payday loans or advances? You can get a portion or all of your directly deposited paycheck up to two days in advance. Think about this, if you decide to get your paycheck two days earlier every time, then isn't it the same as waiting to get it when earned? Here are some pointers on these loans:

- Payday loans are small, expensive loans you repay all at once, typically on your next payday.

- Because they often lead to a cycle of debt, payday loans should be reserved for emergencies.
- There are usually no credit benefits to payday loans, but defaulting can impact your credit score.

And there's this new phenomenon where you can borrow up to $300 to start with no credit check or specific credit score needed. We're just some friendly folks trying to help out the little people. Then, if you pay that back on time, these good folks are willing to up the ante and lend you $500 now. This can go on to where you may be able to borrow a few thousand dollars, but read the fine print. Interest rates are high and penalties even worse. While this is new to us in America, it has been going on for a while around the world. Again, can you think of a way this will make your life better in the long term? If you're within a few hundred dollars from disaster, you need to seek help right away.

Lastly, are you still not sure if big brother is listening? Go ahead, name something you'd like to buy out loud, or something you looked for online, and watch how you start to see ads popping up on your phone, in your email, and on your social accounts. We have been trained to be consumers, and we're so good at it we're willing to go into debt to prove it. And why are we so willing? Status! We believe that money is the true indicator of just how smart and powerful a person is. While I can't argue that money is powerful, I can say without a doubt, it can have little to do with how smart a person is. Of course there are exceptions, as there are to most anything, but I've been surrounded with wealthy people, and for some folks it's just plain luck. Some have it, and some don't. You probably have heard the term "golden touch," and I have seen this many times. I know many traders, and there's no shortage that think they are extremely intelligent based on the money they have made. But after the pits closed, many of those have not been able to translate that success into another financially successful career. It is said that money makes you more of who you really are. If you're not a genuinely nice person, more money will only make you less nice and vice versa. You've seen this, or will, at some point in your life I assure you.

I will say this once again, when you acquire control over your money and spending habits, life will show you it has so much more to enjoy. But don't forget to do your homework. So many of the techniques used to get us to buy are based on the fact that we just won't spend any time researching or learning more before we spend.

eight

Did I Win?

EVERYONE HAS A CHOICE ON HOW THEY LIVE, BUT VERY FEW know what to do, especially financially. We don't teach that often enough, nor do we start early enough.

My good friend Burt Levy said to me the other day, "Instead of trying to leave a better world for our children, why don't we bring better ones into it?" A novel idea, Burt.

Remember when we were young, we would often get asked what we wanted to be when we grew up? Do you ever recall any ten-year-olds saying they wanted to be rich? Maybe, but I don't recall that being an answer. Yet, as we get out into the real world, we've been trained to believe that money solves all problems. If we only had enough money, we'd be happy. And that is how money gains control of our decisions, making us believe it is the solution to happiness.

While most people will never admit to chasing the almighty dollar, many have fallen into that trap. Their happiness is based on the pursuit of money or on how much they have in their bank account. The idea being that if you make more money, you'll be happier. Mostly because that means you can buy more stuff, live in a bigger home, drive a fancier car, and so on. Or is it more about how we want others to perceive us? In my experience, I've rarely seen a person who makes a lot of money be happier. I've heard that money simply makes you more of who you really are. I come from the trading pits of Chicago and have seen some folks do very well, while others crashed and burned. Many of the people I worked with who made a great deal of money developed problems they hadn't anticipated, like drug addiction, alcoholism, and depression. These often led to relationship problems at home, divorce, and even suicide. So, you've got to ask yourself, is the pursuit of money the main factor in creating a better life? I admit that being broke is no great way to live, but the choice to never be broke again is within your grasp if you learn and practice how to control money. There are moments in life that happen, many times with family or friends, that don't cost much money but have a deep impact on your emotional well-being. These are moments that you can never get back, but how can you enjoy such moments if you're always concerned about money? Think about it, are the best times in your life generated by how much money you have in your bank account? Maybe it is, but I truly hope not, because what I've seen and learned is that money by itself doesn't make you happier. Don't get me wrong, having little to no money is no fun. I'm just saying that it is not the end-all-be-all path to happiness. I am also saying that when you learn to control your spending habits and choose the best practices to handle what funds you have, you will find many aspects of life more enjoyable. Read that again as it's a mouthful.

The book began by providing you with a method in which you can start to gain control of your financial situation, by learning how you spend your hard earnings and what triggers you to so readily hand those earnings out. This is really the key to getting yourself into a position of control, and I assure you, you will not only see it, but you'll feel it as well. But, you also need to do your due diligence. By that I mean do your homework on things you purchase and invest in. And keep in mind that price does not always dictate quality, as more often it is determined by brand or marketing.

A friend of mine recently asked me if I could tell the difference between a watch that costs $500 and one that costs $5,000. I said other than cost, I have no idea. He laughed as he said that is often the only difference. It had nothing to do with quality. That's not to say that there aren't very high-quality watches and those made with inferior craftsmanship and parts. But you get the point. You can buy a diamond at a discount store, or you can go to Tiffany's. I know, you're going to say that with diamonds it's all about cut, color/clarity, and carat weight. As mentioned in chapter one, Nicky Oppenheimer, chair of De Beers Diamonds, once said, "Diamonds are intrinsically worthless, except for the deep psychological need they fill."

It's your psychological need that's causing you financial issues, and that's what you need to change if you desire to live a better life.

Once you understand that you can control your financial situation, it will allow you to develop more skills, like setting financial goals—starting with your short-term ones and moving to the longer-term ones. Create a plan, build an emergency fund, manage debt, or even seek professional help. What I'm saying is that there's a natural flow to understanding how money works, and then there are steps to help you gain that control of your overall financial situation. You don't always need a professional to help you gain control; you simply need the desire, self-discipline, and to do your own work.

I had a fellow financial literacy friend tell me the other day that he learned 72 percent of employed people expect their employer to help with their financial well-being, and this doesn't mean higher pay. My first question was "Why would people expect their employer to teach them about money?" If I'm hiring people, it's to do a specific job, not so I can teach financial literacy on my time and dime. That may come across as cold, but what these folks are saying is that they have not taken any steps on their own to learn because they expect someone else to actively reach out and teach them. For free.

I often ask myself that if money is such a major part of our lives from birth to death, and with all the problems it brings, why don't people try to learn more about it? You cannot sit around waiting for someone else to fix your troubles. You need to live your life with intent and get out there and do it for yourself. It will prove very rewarding.

This book's purpose is to open your eyes to the possibilities in life and show you how to go after that feeling of happiness in ways that won't come from simply having more money.

I completely understand that things like debt, credit, or how credit scores really are made and used may not be the most exciting things for you. But wait until you get into investing and finding out your risk tolerance. Now that will be fun, right?

Okay, so you're not a numbers or financial person, which is why you really need to determine whether money controls you or you control it. Then you can determine the life you want to live. Now it's your choice, and you must live with the consequences of that decision. This is why I'm telling you things they don't tell you. If you just can't seem to get into the numbers game, you can at least learn how you are controlled and manipulated into spending your money.

Branding and marketing are two things that play an important role in relieving you of your money. The brand Costco reeks of discount, and when we buy from places like this, we believe we are saving money and getting a good deal. And that's true in that Costco does provide quality products at prices better than you may find at your local grocer or wine shop. But we have this mindset that it's better to "pay up" for certain items because we're getting a higher quality product, or it makes us feel better by showing off what we can afford. Take getting a diamond ring, would you rather receive that ring from a discount store or from Tiffany's? How about being the one that gives the ring, would you rather be known for giving that discount diamond, or the person who gave one from Tiffany's? You may "feel" better about giving that Tiffany's ring, but I bet you're still cringing at the price you paid. And in all honesty, it is a diamond ring either way.

Isn't it funny how there are times we are thrilled at getting a discount and other times we look down upon that discounted item? So now comes along that marketing strategy that works to provide you with a sense of getting a high-quality product for a great price. Or the message could be that if you drive this car, you're making this statement about your financial well-being. The idea is often that if you purchase this product, you'll be stating you're living a certain lifestyle. And we love that idea, so we buy into it readily. Remember when I mentioned we all judge those around us? You know, by the clothes we wear, car we drive, house we own (after 158 more payments), and we come to some determination that that person must be well-off and very smart. And if I spend my money on those things, I'll look well-off and smart too. Once you learn and start to take control of your financial well-being, you'll look at those folks differently. That person may look car rich, but they may be cash poor. Would you rather be cash rich and drive a more suitable car that shows you're not falling for the trap of spending all your money, or have all those fancy things and be stressing every day about what little money you have? It's what we typically do, and we have the power to change that.

Money is a tool that we need to learn how to better use to reach our goals in life. And like many tools we own, it's not brought out and used every day on things that don't need fixing. Do you ever ask yourself when purchasing something, do I really need that, or why am I buying this? Question yourself, develop a sense of purpose with your buying power, and spend with intent.

The interesting thing about money is it doesn't care who you are, what car you drive, what house you own, your gender, color, religion, culture, or anything at all. It doesn't even care about other money. Maybe that's why we want it so badly, because we all seem to want what we can't have. Wouldn't it be great if we were just happy with what we already have?

This book was not written to tell you what to do with your money, or how to live your life. That's your choice. But I believe if you gain control of your money, you'll see there is much more that life has to offer, and you'll be much better off mentally and physically.

So, did I win? Only you can determine that.

It is my sincerest wish that this book will help you live a more meaningful, healthier, and happier life. Go live your life with intent!

Your Choice

IT REALLY DOESN'T MATTER WHERE YOU ARE NOW FINANCIALLY. I know people of all backgrounds and income levels where money still controls them. You never seem to have enough or always want more, and that affects your ability to enjoy what life really has to offer. Personally, I'd rather spend time with my family and friends over a cold beer than be in a room full of people trying to prove how smart and wealthy they are. But that's me. Maybe you enjoy the part of life that is all about chasing the almighty dollar, and I understand how intoxicating that can be from my days in the trading pits. If that's your choice then I suggest you put yourself in a position where money comes your way, as opposed to always chasing it. Again, it's a mindset and you might consider giving it some thought.

It doesn't matter where you're starting from. It's more important that you get started. I know it's one thing to say you're going to make a change and another to stick with it until you start seeing results, and that takes time. You've spent a lifetime making financial decisions that have gotten you to where you are today, so making a change won't be easy. Much like a New Years resolution that typically fails, you don't want to fall back into your old habits. Have you ever tried quitting something you really enjoyed doing, like smoking or drinking alcohol? It's not easy to change your habits and that has a lot to do with your desire to change. First and foremost, you must WANT to make the change, and that's based on your belief the change will be beneficial. Have you ever noticed when you want something bad enough, you'll find a way to get it? How many of you have spent more on a car than you had originally planned? This car is all I need, but that car is what I really want, and that's the one you end up bringing home. This is a pattern that keeps you from gaining control and still living paycheck to paycheck.

An example of this is in my very own neighborhood. All the homes have three car garages, and yet many homes are unable to fit their cars in those garages because the people living there have so much stuff that they use the garage for storage space. It probably holds true in your neighborhood too. It's said that rich people buy time, while poor people buy stuff. The stuff they buy provides a short-term feeling of joy. If you understand the money you spend provides only short-term happiness, you may start re-thinking your buying habits.

Here's something I haven't mentioned before: Receiving and Giving money. When we're young, we love to receive money (okay, I'm not sure there's ever a time in life we don't enjoy receiving money), but when we're older we learn the joy of giving. Christmas is our favorite time to be thankful for what we have, including the ability to give and receive. If you have young children, there's nothing more enjoyable than watching them open their gifts on Christmas morning. But let me ask you a question; how do you determine the cost of the gift you're giving? What's more important when making this decision; the cost to you, or the object you're giving? We've all seen movies where the mom or dad chase all over town looking for that one gift their child says they want most from Santa. And they're willing to pay over the asking price to get it. What does that teach your child, and what does that say about you? Many of us have post-Christmas remorse regarding the amount of money we've spent. But it's okay because we put it all on the credit card and can pay it off slowly, might I add, with interest. You've just obligated incidental money that is now unavailable until the bills are paid off. This can spiral into having less to spend as using credit becomes more common. Remember, you're accustomed to having X amount of dollars to spend on incidentals, and you're not about to change that habit now.

Have you ever received a gift that cost you money? Gift cards are an easy way to provide a gift that the one receiving can determine what to spend it on, relieving the giver of the concern they bought the wrong gift. Here's the thing, I've received many gift cards in my lifetime. Let's say it's a $100 card to a restaurant. The problem is it costs $200 to dine at that restaurant. Or let's say you receive a gift card for $100 at Best Buy and you go there to shop for something you want or need. Do you say, "I'm only spending $100," or does the little devil on your shoulder tell you to buy whatever you want because you're getting $100 off the price? Again, this behavior causes you to spend more of your money.

Don't think for a minute those gift cards weren't meant to get you in the store or shopping online where they know you're likely to spend more than the value of the card.

This brings me back to "Pay Attention." You must be constantly on the lookout for these kinds of tactics that are designed to relieve you from your hard-earned money. Take the very popular word "sale;" it has a special trigger for many of us, as we believe that means we're getting a deal. If that's on something you've really wanted, there's no stopping you from getting it once it's on sale. I have friends that love to "stock up" on items when a sale is going on at the grocery store. Remember I discussed those wonderful coupons? These good folks may have two refrigerators, two freezers, and a big pantry fully loaded with goods, and yet they still buy more simply because there's a sale. You know what I'm talking about, just look in your closet at the amount of clothes and shoes you have. I bet many of those were purchased while on sale. I'm not saying that buying things on sale is bad, just that you need to be aware if this is a trigger for you.

One other subject to bring up before I close is our ability to rationalize. We start this thought process at a very early age, where we learn to provide a great excuse (er, I mean explanation) as to why we need to buy that object. In fact, we get extremely good at it as we grow older. Funny thing is, it's easy to see another trying to rationalize, but rarely in ourselves, as we believe we're very good at it. And you may be, but it doesn't change the fact that you're determined to get what you want, whatever the cost.

Let's wrap this up and get you on track:
Free will is defined as "the power of acting without the constraint of necessity or fate; the ability to act at one's own discretion." In other words, it's your choice in what you do with your life and how each decision you make will affect your life. There are those who are obsessed with the choices they make and those that are more carefree, often having the "it is what it is" attitude. When I plan, I almost always consider how my decisions will impact the ability to accomplish my goals; myself personally, my family especially, and possibly the organization I'm representing. To be fair, I don't use this criterion for every single decision, but if you do it often enough it becomes a habit, and decisions are made with greater intent using less effort.

So, what do I mean by that? I mean that if you truly wish to take control of any aspect of your life you must start by recognizing the need and then creating the desire to make a change. I discussed the idea of setting goals financially, so how about starting with a simple goal of what your life might look like if money were not an issue? I'm not talking about winning the lottery or a life event that provides an influx of newfound money. I'm talking about making a commitment to learning more about your relationship with it, and how you may be able to enjoy a better life by doing so. We all have friends we know, like, and trust, as we also have those friends we know, but don't like or trust. The more you know, like, and trust your decisions with money, the better your relationship with it.

I wish you happiness and success in life!

Acknowledgments

WHEN ASKED ABOUT ACKNOWLEDGMENTS MY FIRST thought was how does one acknowledge all the people that got you to where you are today? I don't know if everything happens for a reason, but as I look back on those (the ones I can remember) who were instrumental to my growth, I do so in hopes that someday they'll know just what a difference they made. As for those who worked to hold me back, thank you, as it only made me stronger.

Funny how this even got started. One day I was on a call with my friend Jeff Schwartz, and he mentioned something to me that started this whole new outlook for what I was trying to do. He told me how much he loved the way I live my life with intent. And everything since that conversation has involved living with intention. One sentence is all it took to start my new media company, a new podcast, some public speaking, and the writing of this book.

We're often asked, "What or who inspired you when you were younger, and what or who inspires you now?" I had no superhero or athlete or anyone I really looked up to and wanted to aspire to be as I grew up. But I can now say I get inspiration from just about everyone around me. Every conversation has a message in it, as my good friend Sir Billy Dorsey recently pointed out. Thank you, Billy, you are the definition of inspiration.

But inspiration comes in many forms. Like from the people that surround me wanting and wishing me success and providing incredible support. Folks like JW Wilson, PJ Ewing, Scott Lask, Dan Coakley, Gene Carr, Trunnis Goggins, and the whole GLMV Chamber membership. There are folks that have long believed in me even after many, many, failures: especially friends like Jim Norman and Mike Tobin.

Then there are some special people that show up in your life just when you need them. Folks like Ret. Chief Master Sergeant USAF David Nordel (thank you for sharing your publisher) and my dear friend Jan Barlow who took it upon herself to make sure I stayed on track.

Lastly, those extra special people that have been with you all your meaningful life. Casey, Liam, and Kate, you each have inspired me and shown incredible support in times I'm not sure I deserved. You continue to inspire me, and many of those around you (though you don't always see that) with the way you live and help others. I am so proud.

And to all those I have not mentioned, those of you who jumped in to provide support in any way, all the while knowing I could barely afford to pay attention much less for your services, I can't thank you enough.

God bless all of those who have touched my life.

About the Author

With over 38 years of experience in the financial world, Bill Haase has a background of 20 years in the trading pits of Chicago (Wall Street), processing and underwriting of loans with major banks, and several years of financial advising (Main Street) to people like you. While he was never a trader (but *was* a broker!), Bill exercised occasional trades, and was involved in the transactions of stocks, stock options, Bonds, S&P futures, foreign currencies, risk arbitrage, and interest rate futures that included Eurodollars, Euroyen, and Libor. In 2004, Bill was the first person in the US to execute side-by-side pit and computer trading at the same time. No amusement park will ever develop a ride like Bill had on that day! He also had a 4-year running radio show titled "Innovative Strategies," where Bill and his guests discussed financial literacy and how to build a business from

concept to success. Logging nearly 1000 interviews including a couple hundred live on the show, Bill is launching a
podcast with special guests to discuss how they live their
lives with intention, and what parts they live by default.

Bill began his career at the Chicago Board Options
Exchange (CBOE) as a runner with Goldberg Brothers taking option orders on stocks to the various brokers in the
pits and acting as the runner when those options were
executed. When hired, Bill was told that only one out of ten
runners would make it a full month; yet Bill lasted twenty
years. From there, Bill graduated to buying and selling
stocks for traders as they hedged their options positions.
About a year and a half into this crazy world, the powers
that be thought Bill might be a good fit working in the Ivy
Tower helping with a relatively new strategy called Risk
Arbitrage. Bill participated in selling or buying baskets of
stock that could be valued as high as $15,000,000 each, and
the trade would be completed in a matter of minutes. Back
then, there was a person who would execute (trade) futures
against the stock position (if buying stocks, then selling
futures and vice versa) that was chosen and lock in the
difference in pricing. This was primarily the Fortune 500
stocks versus the S&P 500 futures, but other options were
used occasionally. One day, Bill was sent to have lunch with
Prudential Bache, and signed the largest stock loan contract
of its day for $100 million. However, Bill longed to get back
to the action of the pits, recalling the mantra, "You either
love it or hate it, and you'll know quickly."

Bill headed over to the Chicago Mercantile Exchange

and worked a desk with a well-known company called Drexel Burnham Lambert Inc. in the Eurodollar pit (interest rate futures). This was the largest trading pit in the world with roughly 1500 people at any given time, trading over 40 different futures and any combination of those futures, as well as the options on those futures. Just nine months into this new gig, Drexel got forced into bankruptcy in 1990 for an issue with Junk Bonds, and after a bit Bill wound up at Nikko Securities as the desk manager for a group of Japanese brokers. A little over six years later, Bill switched sides and moved into the pit as a clerk involved with spreads (buying one contract while selling another at the same time, which could involve strategies for spreading that may include several futures at once). About four years later, computer trading had finally made it to the US. What a splash this made!

When your world gets taken over by technology where does one go? Certainly not the corporate world, or so he thought. While trying to start his own business, Bill landed at Chase Bank in Milwaukee processing loan modifications, moving back to Illinois a year later with Bank of America processing and underwriting loans for residential deals. After three years, Bill became a financial advisor and worked for various companies, recounting how his past experiences would help him get a step ahead of the competition.

What Bill learned was that most people didn't understand much of about how to develop individual and family portfolios. Bill found this frustrating, in that he knew he could help, but they just couldn't understand the intricacies of how money works. Bill discovered his desire to teach financial literacy and launched his radio show that included how to build a business from concept to success. With so many people leaving their corporate jobs, many would embark on their own with no idea of what they were getting into. Four years later, Bill made the pivot to launch a podcast that mimicked his public speaking with a focus on financial literacy. This led him to write this book.

Bill was called to provide basic knowledge and show people how they can take back control with a little effort and a desire to live a better life. This book is for those who wish to stop letting money stress them out and live in peace the rest of their lives.